MW01101936

Our Faith Renewed

SaraBeth Vaughn
with Nat Davis

CROSSBOOKS
PUBLISHING

CrossBooks™
A Division of LifeWay
1663 Liberty Drive
Bloomington, IN 47403
www.crossbooks.com
Phone: 1-866-879-0502

Scripture taken from the King James Version of the Bible.

Scriptures taken from the Holy Bible, New International Version®, NIV®. Copyright © 1973, 1978, 1984, 2011 by Biblica, Inc.™ Used by permission of Zondervan. All rights reserved worldwide. www.zondervan.com The "NIV" and "New International Version" are trademarks registered in the United States Patent and Trademark Office by Biblica, Inc.™ All rights reserved.

Some names have been changed to protect the privacy of individuals.

First published by CrossBooks 03/14/2014

ISBN: 978-1-4627-3589-1 (sc)
ISBN: 978-1-4627-3590-7 (hc)
ISBN: 978-1-4627-3588-4 (e)

Library of Congress Control Number: 2014905006

Printed in the United States of America.

This book is printed on acid-free paper.

CONTENTS

FOREWORD

"By faith..." (Hebrews 11)

I would like to start by saying I am humbled and privileged to be asked by my dear friends Rob and SaraBeth Vaughn to write the foreword for "Our Faith Renewed."

Faith Mackenzie Vaughn may have only been in this world for forty-two minutes on May 19, 2011, but she has had one of the greatest impacts on my life of any person I have ever known. My Lord Jesus Christ uses "forty-two minutes of Faith" continually as a reminder to demonstrate faith in every area of my life.

I chose Hebrews 11 and the words "by faith" because those words came to mind regularly throughout SaraBeth's pregnancy with Faith. Rob and SaraBeth were told early and often that this pregnancy was going to be difficult and abortion should be considered. However, abortion not being an acceptable option, by faith they endured. The months were filled with good news and bad, ups and downs, trials and tribulations. The doctors had no definite answers but most advised that nothing good would come of continuing their pregnancy. The Great Physician, however, had a plan and continually showed His power.

You may be asking yourself what kind of plan includes a forty-two minute life, and where is the power or the good? Faith is now in heaven resting safe from any harm, pain, suffering or sin, proving that we know that all things work together for good to them that love

God, to them who are the called according to His purpose. God will continue to use Faith's precious life in a powerful way because she is committed to Him by faith.

It is my hope that everyone who reads this book will realize that it is by God's plan and His power that they have this inspiring story of faith to read. I also pray that you see the need for Jesus Christ in your life, commit to His plan, and live renewed by Faith.

Pastor Bryan Volpe

Acknowledgements

This book, our story and Baby Faith would not have been possible without the love, grace and mercy of my Lord and Savior, Jesus Christ. To Him be all the glory for the life of Faith, and all that He has done in and through our lives.

My precious husband and children have been relentless in encouraging me and keeping me going during the times I wanted to quit. Thank you for putting up with me and allowing me time to spend at my computer writing this story. I couldn't have done it without you.

My parents have been the financial backbone of this project, as well as a source of encouragement. Thank you for making this possible.

Nat Davis was a God-send. She took my words and my writing, and made them into something beautiful. She pushed me and encouraged me, and most of all, she inspired me to stay the course. This project wouldn't be in existence without her willingness to step out in faith and work so hard to see this to completion.

My very dear friends, Holly Banner and Carrie Mizell, took precious hours out of their very busy schedule to read and edit our manuscript. Thank you for the blessing of your friendship.

Notes from the Authors

I have never aspired to write a book, and "author" was never on my list of dream careers. But through this journey, God laid it on my heart to share our story with anyone who would listen. If there is one message I want to convey through this book, it is this: God is good, all the time. Even in the midst of the most painful trial imaginable, He shows up in big ways, and beyond measure blesses those who are obedient to Him.

It is my prayer that as you read our story, you open your hearts to what He has to say to you. I can tell you that the woman who signed up to go to Nicaragua is not the woman who is sharing her heart with you. The Holy Spirit has lit a fire in my soul, and has given me a passion to tell everyone who will hear just how great He is.

I am forever changed by His faithfulness, and by the little girl He chose to be our daughter. Rob and I count it an honor that He chose us to walk this road, to be able to tell you of His love. May God bless you and keep you as you step into our lives and see how our "Faith" has been renewed.

SaraBeth Vaughn

When I first took this project, it was little more than "just another job." I have been a freelancer for a few years now, and in that time have written hundreds of articles.

None have had the effect that this one has had. This quickly became more than just another project. It was a life story, one that has had a huge impact. It has been a pleasure getting to know SaraBeth and hear her story. There is nothing like seeing a story, not as just words in a book, but through their own eyes, seeing it as they saw it, feeling what they felt. In every word, I felt their hurt, their deep-seated pain, all woven together with that scarlet thread of redemption. There is great heartache in this story, but also a greater intimacy for it, a deeper understanding of both life and the love and grace of God.

I hope that this story will reach others the way it has reached me.

Nat Davis is a freelance writer, editor, and promoter. She has written hundreds of articles and has been privileged to be the editor on a number of books, many of which are now available on Amazon and other venues. You can find more about her from her Facebook page- search "Davis Professionals" to see her latest updates.

Chapter One

PRELUDE

The casket was way too small. No casket could ever be that tiny.

And yet... it *was*.

I suppressed a sob and wrenched my eyes away. Rob needed me. My children needed me. My children... *Faith*...

I pretended to read the program, although I had long since memorized it. The thin paper crumpled in my shaking fingers, and the ink blurred. Her name, written in beautiful font, dissolved and spread across the page, a bleeding stain that matched the hole in my heart. I blinked, and the words realigned, never having moved in the first place.

Once again, I felt my eyes drawn to the casket. My eyes remained fixed on that small wooden box as Bryan stepped up to the platform behind it. His voice breaking just slightly, he gripped the edge of the pulpit and spoke.

"I would like to start by saying what a privilege it is to know Rob and SaraBeth, their children, their family and friends; and to be welcomed into such an exceptional family. I would also like to say what an honor it has been to experience with them the story and life of Faith."

I closed my eyes as our best friend gave his thoughts.

"I'm reminded today of one of my favorite chapters from Scripture, Hebrews 11. Two words in Hebrews 11 stand out to me. Those words are, "by faith." As each of us commit to memory this chapter of our lives, let it be said that by faith, Rob and SaraBeth Vaughn demonstrated to us and the world true Christian faith. The word 'Christian' means to be Christ-like; like Christ, when faced with His death, He prayed, 'Father, if thou be willing, remove this cup from me, nevertheless, not My will but Thine be done,' then laid down his life to provide salvation to everyone who will believe in Him. Rob and SaraBeth have demonstrated through faith an unfailing trust in God with the life of their child, wanting her life and story to bring their family, friends, and the world to salvation through Jesus Christ. And for that, they will always be remembered by me, and I pray by you, as heroes of faith."

Bryan's voice broke slightly, and there was a pause. Swallowing, he then continued. He unfolded a piece of paper and began to read. "I will now read a letter to Faith from her parents..."

Working to steady his voice, Bryan read the words that my husband and I had penned together. These words carried our fears and dreams, and the hopes on which they rode. They held the promise that we clung to so desperately, the knowledge that we would see our beloved little girl again. This time, it would be for good. There would be no goodbyes.

Bryan concluded the letter and stepped down. His steps were echoed by the beginning strains of a song penned for such a moment as this. Our friend Kelly is a talented artist, and she sang beautifully that day. She sang the song that carried me through these past few months. Her voice rang out, clear and composed- but her red-rimmed eyes revealed her sorrowed heart.

There were photographs I wanted to take,
Things I wanted to show you;

There was so much I wanted to do, so much that I would miss...I would never sing a lullaby late at night to a fussy newborn. I would never read bedtime stories to her, or watch her take her first steps.

People say that I am brave but I'm not-
Truth is, I'm barely hanging on...

I was barely hanging on, but I knew I was relying on the strength of One greater than me.

The words flowed through the auditorium, soothing the hearts of those present. They wrapped themselves around my own heart, and I could feel the truth in them. Even in these dark days, the Lord's promises held true. I could feel His arms around me now, holding me, carrying me through.

Kelly continued to sing, but my mind began to wander. This song held the truth of my entire pregnancy. When we first received Faith's diagnosis, we had bought a CD containing that song, and it was the same song that carried us through. When we began to plan her services in anticipation of her death, I knew right away that we needed to play this song.

As Kelly sang, I remembered each and every detail of my pregnancy, turning them over in my mind as though they were precious stones. I reminisced every moment, every hope and heartbreak. I told myself in a repeating refrain that even though I loved her, no one could love her like Jesus. I felt as though I had accomplished a great task that the Lord had given me. I carried her, loved her, and did everything humanly possible to fight for her life.

I closed my eyes, remembering. The church, the people around me began to fade as I went back, back to when I first learned of my pregnancy.

I stared down at the test in my hands, hardly daring to breathe. Two pink lines stared back at me, faint but defiant of all our hopes and expectations. Finally sucking in a lungful of air, I hurried through the house in search of my husband, who was in the kitchen making dinner.

"Rob!" Rob looked up, startled, as I thrust the test in front of him. His hands flinched away from it as if it were poison. Well, I *had* just peed on it, after all. "Is there a second line, or am I imagining it?"

Gingerly leaning forward, avoiding any possible contact with the stick, he peered at the results window. I waited anxiously, biting my nails in anticipation. After a moment, he looked back up at me. "Is this thing even right?"

It wasn't the answer I was looking for, but it was answer enough. I was pregnant with our third child.

I called the doctor the next day to schedule an appointment, and they scheduled me to come in a few days later to meet with the nurse. Pregnancy tests are not infallible, after all. The pregnancy was confirmed, much to my relief. I'd been so afraid that I would not have another child.

My parents were the first to know the news. We dressed our younger daughter, SaraGrace, in a t-shirt that read, "MID'L SISTER" and we headed over to my parents. They were ecstatic, and my mom cried. I then shared the news with my sisters, including my baby sister, who was also pregnant. Kiss and Beas were overjoyed. I couldn't help but apologize to Beas, five months pregnant at the time. Excited as I was about my own news, I didn't want to feel like I was invading her spotlight. Of course, there was no need, since she wasn't upset anyway.

Next was my best friend, Amy, who was always there for me through everything. Her support would become invaluable to me in the next few months, along with that of my own family.

I look back on these memories with a bittersweet sadness. These euphoric days are a balm to my soul, remembering a time when we were only excited by the prospect of having another child. Who knew the dark days that would come ahead?

Rob and I had long debated the size of our family. He originally wanted four to five kids until SaraGrace became so very independent. It was then that he changed his mind to sticking with the two that we had. For the longest time, I was okay with that. But the more I thought about it, I just did not feel like our family was complete. We didn't really NEED any more children. Our two are a handful, and let's be honest, it takes a village!

It also takes a money tree, and ours had withered and died. My hours had been cut, SaraGrace started school (an added monthly expense), and to add to that, we had to start driving separately because of my hours. To adjust, I took a shift that would coincide with my children's school days, allowing me to pick them up from school after work.

Despite this adjustment, it was still a lot of driving, which meant we had to buy more gas. It was just one more added expense on our already-burdened budget. Nothing really pointed in the direction that we were ready for another child. Nothing, except for God's plan!

It was definitely an added burden, but God knew what He was doing. Jeremiah 29:11 later became our life verse for Faith- "For I know the plans I have for you," declares the Lord. "Plans to prosper you, not to harm you. Plans to give you hope and a future" (NIV). Our path was ordered long before we knew it was. We did not know the end of our story, but the Lord called it an "expected" end. He knew what was going to happen, and had called it for our good!

Chapter Two

IN THE BEGINNING

It was certainly God's plan when I first met SaraBeth, though I didn't know it then. We met at a nightclub on a Thursday night, ladies' night.

I was living a very different lifestyle at that time. I had learned early on how to win the way to a girl's heart, and I used it to my advantage. My brother had first shown me a Playboy picture when I was very young, about 6 or 7. At the time, I did not know how this would affect me. As I grew older, I began to see women as little more than my own personal playthings. I would get what I wanted, and then I would toss them aside.

I also enjoyed partying. I started drinking heavy around the age of 15. If I didn't get it from my own parents, I would find a man at the gas station to buy it for me. I would give him some money in exchange. In middle school and throughout high school, I partied with my friends. It wasn't a party unless we had alcohol. This attitude toward women, partying, and alcohol would set a horrible trend for my life.

I was only 19 when I married my first wife. A year into our marriage, we started to attend church. Up to this point, I didn't know anything about God or what He had done for me. All I knew was that my mom would sit with me at night when I was a kid and we would pray for our family.

Now, years later, going to church for the first time scared the crap out of me. People who went to church were good people and God loves people like that. I knew I was not one of those people.

Well, I somehow made it through that first service. The roof didn't fall and there was no lightning strike. I lived, and even continued to go to church. I learned that if you don't ask Jesus in to your heart, you would go to hell. I didn't know anything about a relationship with Christ.

I know the difference now. I know that the difference is that Jesus can come into your heart, but He doesn't just want your heart. He wants a relationship with you. He wants to know you, and for you to know Him. That is the real difference. It is in knowing how He works, what He wants, and what He did for you and me.

Going to church for the first time, I encountered Christ. I did what they told me to do. I said the prayer and I was baptized- but I wasn't truly saved. I just wanted the fire insurance.

Sometime later, I divorced my wife. We had been married less than three years. I was a terrible husband who wanted to party more than I wanted to be married- and party I did.

It was this same lifestyle that led me to the woman I would marry for life. When I asked her to dance, I did so because I thought she was pretty. I had no idea that it would be a major turning point in my life.

We had been dating for only six weeks before she moved in with me. Her parents didn't like it, but we were young and didn't care. A few short months later, we were married.

I married SaraBeth, but my partying went on. I was a partier, and being married wasn't going to change that. To this day, I honestly don't know how she put up with me. I would stay out with the guys until 2 or 3 AM, drinking heavily the whole time. It was *bad enough that I would end up with a nose bleed sometimes. Blood would pour from my nose, but still I didn't stop.*

God was laying a path for my life, but I couldn't see it then. I was only focused on what I wanted. I wanted to have fun, and nothing was going to get in the way of that.

Then we received the news that I wasn't expecting.

SaraBeth was pregnant.

Learning that I was pregnant was a shock to me. In my first marriage, I had had trouble getting pregnant. I took a cycle of fertility medication, and then they started doing some testing.

That's when I learned that I had a bicorneate and septate uterus. This is an abnormality in the shape of the uterus; depending on the severity of the diagnosis, it could severely affect pregnancies.

A bicorneate uterus has a deep indentation at the top of the uterus wall. Normally, the uterus is shaped like a pear, but in my case, the indentation caused it to form the shape of a heart.

A septate uterus has a dividing wall down the center. It may be only a partial wall, or it may extend as far down as the cervix, called a complete septate. Mine was complete.

The first diagnosis wasn't too bad. It would come up during ultrasounds for my later pregnancies, but it was only an observation the technician would make. It didn't really affect anything.

The second one, however, was the one that made things complicated. At the time, however, other things were taking priority in my mind and I didn't think much of it. I was going through a divorce, and the thought of getting pregnant didn't really enter my mind. I knew that I'd had a hard time getting pregnant, but after my divorce, I didn't really expect that I would ever have children.

When I met Rob, I told him that we would never be able to have children. At the time, it mattered little to him. Having children was not on his agenda; he was a partier, and just wanted someone to do things with. We did everything together.

Shortly after we had married, I began to feel ill. I had all the typical pregnancy symptoms, but I knew it was impossible. The thought never crossed my mind that I could be with child. My mother insisted something was wrong and that I needed to get my blood checked. My father jokingly said, "You're sure you're not pregnant?"

But it was impossible.

Around that time, we went on a trip with my family. It was fall, and we were at a hunting camp in Plains, GA, for Thanksgiving. Instead of the traditional Thanksgiving dinner, all I wanted was homemade macaroni and cheese with turkey gravy on it. Yes, it was strange. I was having the classic pregnancy cravings, but still the thought did not enter my mind.

I lay in bed that night with my husband, still feeling nauseated. I remember telling Rob, "I don't know what I have gotten into, but I feel horrible." I didn't know if it was a stomach bug, or maybe food poisoning. Whatever it was, I had it bad.

The day after Thanksgiving, we were shopping at the mall. We had to make a detour to the bathroom, which required walking through the baby section. I remember looking at all of those tiny clothes, wishing I could experience that one day.

When we got back home later that week, I reluctantly took the test. No one really suspected that I might be pregnant. They joked about it, but it always was a joke in our family. I really believed we would never have children. I took it just to be sure, to rule out the possibility. But even as I went through the motions required for the test, I knew it couldn't happen. There was that diagnosis...

I took the test, and instantly the results lay before me, undeniable.

The impossible had happened. I was carrying a child in my womb.

Chapter Three

A BUDDING FAMILY

Being a dad was new to me. I didn't know how to be one, and I was scared. My father wanted nothing to do with me when I was growing up. I knew little of him until I was about 6 years old. I knew of him, but I didn't really know anything about him up until this point. My mother had remarried, and at that time she started planning trips to my father's house. I remember one trip I stayed the entire weekend by myself. The only time I spent with my father was the trip home.

I didn't know it then, but these childhood experiences would have a huge impact on me as an adult. Shortly after my marriage to my first wife, we moved to Gainesville to be near my father, who I still didn't really know that much. The move proved to be not worth the effort, it seemed to me. I couldn't do anything right, and he told me how much I reminded him of my mother. Obviously, this wasn't a good thing. Every time I came around, I got the feeling I wasn't wanted, so I slowly stopped coming around.

Now, I was faced with this huge responsibility. SaraBeth was pregnant, and I had no idea how to be a father. She had told me when we married that she couldn't get pregnant because she had a problem, so it was never an option that I considered. I didn't care, because I just liked having someone who liked to do the same things I liked to do. We did everything together, not even spending a night away from each other.

It was after Thanksgiving when she finally took a test. She was in the bathroom of our home when the results came back.

"Rob!" From where I stood in the kitchen, I heard her screaming my name. I checked to make sure all the knobs were turned low on the stove before making my way back to the bathroom.

She stood there in that huge bathroom, hands shaking as she held out that white stick. Sure enough, clear as a bell there were two lines. I didn't know what the lines were, but I sure as heck knew what that look on her face meant.

"Oh, crap!" These were the first words out of my mouth. I think she thought that I would be excited, but I was scared to death. How in the world was I supposed to be a father? All I knew was that I didn't want to be like my dad.

The best example I had for being a father was my stepdad, Andy. My mother had remarried when I was young, and he took me in like I was one of his own kids. He had three already, but I was just one more. He and my mom divorced shortly before I met SaraBeth, but I still considered him my dad. To this day, he is still the best father I ever had, and we are still close.

Despite this, he wasn't my father. I knew that. Even then, I thought of him as my real dad. But he wasn't, not really. I came from another man... and what if I turned out to be just like him?

I didn't know what to think. At first, I thought that SaraBeth lied to me. She had told me before that she couldn't have kids. Now here she was- pregnant.

Of course I knew that she wouldn't lie. She wasn't like that. But just at first as the shock came over me, I know the thought crossed my mind. Had she really lied?

I wasn't prepared to be a father, but it was going to happen either way. I didn't know the first thing about what to expect.

I welcomed the pregnancy with open arms. I knew Rob was scared, but for me, it was the fulfillment of a lifelong dream. I'd always wanted children, and to me, there was no greater blessing than to be a mom.

I couldn't tell my parents just yet, but we couldn't hold the news in, either. We had to tell someone. That someone turned out to be Rob's mother.

Immediately after getting the test results, we called her on the phone to share the news. My mother-in-law is not a woman given to overt displays of emotion or excitement. However, she harbors a fierce love for her boys and would do anything for their happiness. So it was that when we told her the news, she did not shout or jump for joy, but said, "If that is what makes you happy, then I am happy."

Despite my joy, I knew that the timing wasn't the greatest, at least for human planning. Rob was attending night school and making an apprentice wage, and I was working for the tax collector. Our "rustic" little house, although cute, was far from romantic, and definitely not the ideal for raising a baby. It was situated in the middle of a field with a dirt driveway. When the rains came, it turned the driveway into a mud bath so thick that I couldn't drive my car. We had the choice of either being stuck, or staying with my parents until the rains let up. Of course, neither option was convenient.

None of that changed the fact that I was definitely pregnant. So began the flurry of doctor's appointments and preparing for a baby. I progressed well enough, with few complications at first. The worst I had to deal with was morning sickness, but that was bad enough. I was sick nearly every day, and I quickly discovered just how ironic the term "morning sickness" really is. It isn't just for the morning!

For some women, morning sickness can last throughout the entire pregnancy. Some find that it wears off halfway through the second trimester. I was one of the lucky ones; by the time I got through my first trimester, the morning sickness had passed.

It was just as good that it did, because I had enough to keep myself occupied. The house we lived in- well, it would work. But it wasn't what we wanted. Of course, you can raise a baby anywhere, really. You don't need a special house or that perfect "nursery." But as first-time parents, we wanted that perfection. This was my dream come true, and I wanted it done right.

But the fact was... we *still* had that house. We were far from stable financially, and it didn't look like things were going to improve any time soon.

Knowing our situation, my parents wanted to be a blessing, and shortly after we shared our joyous news, offered to buy us a house. We spent about two weeks looking. Strange as it sounds, I've never had a thought as to a "dream" home. I was simply content; perhaps it came from never expecting to come across anything grand. Although my parents were buying, Rob and I would be responsible for the taxes on it, so we had to keep that in mind while searching.

We finally found a place just outside of town. It was older and needed updating, but Rob liked it. I had a hard time envisioning what it could be and didn't see much, but I trusted the judgment of my husband and my father. Besides, it was so far from what we had expected that I was just grateful at the opportunity.

It was late in December when we got the keys to the house, and immediately we went to work on the remodel. It was a lot of hard work, and I wasn't exempt. I remember being big and pregnant, scraping vinyl tile off the floor to make way for the new ceramic tile.

The work was slow and I thought we'd never finish, but slowly it came together. I was five months pregnant when we finally moved in, and it wasn't until then that I caught the vision for what this place was. It was the fulfillment of my dream. Everything I ever wanted was embodied in this place. I had my husband, my child, and now a home for my family. We had worked hard to get to this point, but it was worth it.

I look back on that idyllic period with a smile. That short time after we'd moved in was a sweet period. I was seeing the fulfillment of my dream, and I couldn't be more content.

I couldn't imagine what that dream would eventually cost me. I'd always wanted children, but I couldn't begin to realize the trials that lay ahead.

I was 28 weeks along when the complications began. We had been living in that new house for a month and a half.

It was really happening. I was going to be a father. Despite the events of the last nine months, I still couldn't quite believe it. I can't say that I was too excited- it just wasn't real. I'd had nine months to prepare, but I still didn't feel like I was ready.

Ready or not, here it was. I was about to be a father.

Halfway through her pregnancy, we had the appointment to find out what the baby was going to be. When the doctor told us that we were having a boy, that was when I began to get excited. I was grinning from ear to ear. You couldn't have slapped the smile off my face if you tried. Knowing that I was having a son gave me something to look forward to, but I was still scared more than anything.

SaraBeth was 36 weeks when she had Cade. I didn't know anything about a pregnancy or how everything was supposed to go. When the doctors started saying things like "pre-eclampsia" and medical terms like that, I didn't know what to think. I had no idea if it was serious or not. But judging by the doctor's expression as he gave us the news, it wasn't good.

It started with her blood pressure. At first, it was nothing to worry about. She just got the usual warnings from the doctor, and that was it. I was working a lot and still going to school, so SaraBeth went to most of the appointments by herself. We just didn't see why I should need to go. We were new parents, and I didn't know anything about the process, so neither of us could see how me being there would make any difference. At first, it wasn't a big deal. She was progressing fine, other than the blood pressure.

Then it became more. With nearly every appointment, she would end up in the hospital because of the blood pressure. She would call me, and I would go in and sit with her. At the time, I didn't realize how bad it could be. We just had to do what the doctors told us to do.

It was aggravating to me to have all these appointments. As a man, I saw things in black and white. This back and forth stuff wasn't for me. If they said that they would have to make the baby come early, I would be thankful. I'd never really been around kids that much, and I certainly had never seen labor before. How hard could it be? I have a hard time really seeing something before it's there- it's not real to me until I see it. So with that, combined with how much I didn't know, I remained rather disconnected.

SaraBeth was in the hospital for most of the last part of her pregnancy. Her blood pressure was too high at every appointment, and she would always end up in the hospital.

Finally, it all came to an end. SaraBeth went in for an appointment as usual, and they took the tests. This time, we made sure and had our bags with us, just in case. The doctor was running late, so we went across the mall just to kill some time. When we returned an hour later, her numbers had shot up. They were way too high.

The doctor told us that we had played with this for too long and now it was time to deliver. Things moved quickly from there. We went downstairs, and I went into survival mode. My wife would call it "protective daddy mode," but I was just operating without *even thinking about it. I brought the bags in from the car and then helped my wife call her family.*

SaraBeth was scared to death of the C-section, and especially the epidural. She hated needles and would pass out even at the mention of one.

I stayed with her, trying my best to reassure her. She was anxious to meet our new baby, but I just waited. There wasn't much to be excited about just yet. Baby wasn't here yet.

Finally, the doctor was ready. Because of the problems she was having, they decided to do a C-section. They got her ready for the surgery and we were sent to the room.

At 8:22 PM on June 30, 2003, Cade Allan Vaughn was born. I wasn't prepared for the flood of emotions as I watched the doctors pull my son from my wife's stomach.

I was a father.

Chapter Four
MEDI-CADE

I was sort of hoping that after Cade was born, things would begin to change for Rob and me. He would come home early, spend time with his family, become the man I'd always dreamed of. I just knew that when we had Cade, things would change. He would love his son enough to stay home, even if he didn't love me.

When it didn't, I was disappointed, to say the least. This life wasn't what I'd hoped for at all. I wanted Cade to have the perfect life, not parents who couldn't get it together, not knowing if they would even be together from one week to the next.

This was a point of continued contention for us. All he wanted was to party, and nothing I said made any difference. I would nag him about it, a lot. Of course, it did nothing to influence his choices. If anything, it pushed him even further away.

There were other things that added to the stress and drove the wedge in deeper. Rob had gotten a job as an electrician, working a union job. This required him to be on the road for work, and he was gone Monday through Friday. This left me to raise our son by myself.

Difficult enough with any normal child, Cade's medical problems only accentuated it. He was just a few months old when he first developed pneumonia. Little did I know that this would be the first in a long line of illnesses. At six months old, he was diagnosed with RSV. RSV is a respiratory illness similar to bronchitis, and can in fact lead to that diagnosis. In adults, it's similar to just a nasty flu, but RSV can be a serious diagnosis for infants, making it difficult for them to breathe. Ordinarily the doctor would have admitted Cade, but for the fact that the hospital was already full of sick babies.

There was no room at the hospital for Cade. We ended up having to take him home, but set a timer for every 2-4 hours to give him breathing treatments.

From the time he was born, Cade fought sickness. He was on 32 different antibiotics in just 16 months. The pediatrician we had was awful. He refused to consider the option of having tubes put in, and kept prescribing antibiotics. Finally, my father stepped in and scolded me, threatening to beat me if we ever took my son back to that doctor. Of course, I knew he wouldn't actually beat me, but it got his point across well enough.

We knew it was time to switch. The new doctor was a relief. She wasted no time in getting the tubes put in, which helped immensely. She also ordered a round of tests to check for underlying causes such as cystic fibrosis, celiac's, you name it.

They drew his blood and sent it in for tests. Before we got the results back, Sunday came around and we went to church, just as usual. During services, the staff called us to the front, where the deacons gathered around to lay hands and pray over Cade. This turned out to be a miracle in itself. Due to all the doctor's visits, the illnesses, and all his problems, Cade didn't trust a lot of people. He would freak out if you got in his space. But even with all the deacons' hands on him, he just laid there in my arms, not moving. I knew it had to have been of God.

The men prayed for Cade, asking God for healing. Everyone at church knew his story. It was bad enough that he was tagged with nicknames like Medi-Cade and DC (disease carrier) because he was always so sick. But that day at church, God really moved. Two days after that service, we got the test results back. Everything was negative. Cade hasn't been on antibiotics since!

The first two years were a stressful time for me. Not only was I adjusting to being a new mother, I was also having to deal with Cade's almost-constant illnesses.

Finally, I'd had enough. I couldn't do this by myself. With Rob gone all the time, it was up to me to take care of our son. My parents would accompany me to the ER and the hospital with Cade, but Rob was never there because of work.

One of the few times he was able to be there, he watched as they inserted the IV and put the tube down Cade's throat to drain his stomach. Rob couldn't handle it. Cade couldn't stand to have anyone near him, a sad result of so many doctor's visits. He would freak out if they came close, so it took a couple of sticks to insert the IV needle, and then they had to catheterize him.

It was awful to watch. Rob can't handle needles himself, and watching his son go through so much pain was unbearable to him. His reaction upset me, and I shot back, "You think this is hard? Try doing it every time."

I wasn't really trying to be mean, and honestly, I wasn't even angry. If anything, I wrestled with guilt over making such a big deal of his work. I was the mom; it was my job to take care of our son, right? Rob's job was to make a living to provide for his family, which he was doing very well.

Only... the logistics just didn't work. He was providing, but he was gone. And I knew that even while he was out of town, the partying continued. He would work in pairs with his buddies, and after work, they would drink the night away.

Those nights were long for me. As I lay alone in my own bed, I couldn't help but wonder if he was sharing his. In my heart, I didn't think he would really do anything, but still, those long nights created just a whisper of doubt in my mind. But with everything else going on with Cade, I just couldn't question it too deeply. I had so much on my plate that I couldn't begin to question him about it. Even if I did, he would get angry and say that he was tired.

Seeing Cade react at that doctor's visit really got to him. Not too long after, he came home from work one day, only to be called out again the following day. I had reached my breaking point, and I told him I just couldn't do this alone. He needed to stay home. The very next day, instead of going out to the job, he turned in his truck keys.

I have never been so thankful. It was like a ton of bricks had been lifted from my shoulders. Financially, it probably wasn't the best decision, but I needed Rob home with me; finances were the least of my worries. I just knew that with him home, we would be able to work things out- that *I* would be able to work things out. Even then, I had a hard time letting go and letting God.

It was a trying time for all of us. I was trying to be what Cade needed, trying to be a good example to him. I knew that he needed to be raised up to follow Jesus Christ. Rob was trying, too- he went to church with us, things like that. He just didn't have a good moral compass as to what was right and wrong. It didn't help, either, that I had compromised from the beginning- we did meet at a nightclub, after all.

Chapter Five

TIES THAT BIND

Aside from our family and my best friend Amy, no one has been there for us as much as the Volpe family. It started with Sebby and Stacy, the older Volpe couple. They moved in next door to us, and we hit it off right away. I had already crossed paths with them before and knew them, but I had no idea at the time how much of an impact they would have on my life. I knew them from when I was in high school; as part of my school activities, I was involved in showing cattle, and they did the same. Sebby also worked in construction some, which brought him into contact with me through my family's construction business. Besides that, Sebby is also a pastor, and had come to preach a few times at my parents' church.

All of this laid the foundation for a relationship that would soon become an anchor in my life. Rob met them for the first time when they moved in next door. We didn't know anyone around us at the time, so we were just happy to have someone we knew there. They would often invite us over for dinner or just coffee. We would spend hours over there, soaking in their wisdom.

We had done nothing to prevent pregnancy since Cade was born. Quite the opposite, in fact. We tried and tried for another baby.

In early June of 2006, I took a pregnancy test. The results, though positive, were difficult to tell for sure because the lines were very faint. Concerned, I called my doctor, who sent me in for blood work. When the results came back, my numbers were abnormally low, so they had me come in.

As it turned out, I had had an ectopic pregnancy. This is an abnormal pregnancy where the baby is implanted outside the womb. I'd gotten pregnant, alright, but the baby was growing *outside my uterus*! This is nearly always a fatal diagnosis for the baby, and in fact can even be fatal for the mother, as it can lead to life-threatening hemorrhaging.

I was devastated. I had finally begun to accept the thought that we would never have more children. Cade was such a miracle, and it had been so long ago. We had just started to consider that he may be an only child. So when I first got the pregnancy test results back, it revived all those old dreams again, and I wanted nothing more than to have this baby. To lose it so quickly struck a blow to my heart.

I had little time to grieve over it, however. They gave me a medicine to clear my tubes, and we were leaving the very next day to take Cade on a Disney Cruise for his third birthday.

If we're listing faults, I'd be the first to say that one of mine is being a procrastinator. In this case, it served as a good thing. They administered my meds there at the doctor's office and then I went home, fueling my grief into energy as I turned to get everything done before our trip. Bags were packed for the three of us, the paperwork was put in order, and I made sure we had all the essentials for traveling with a toddler. The activity provided a welcome distraction, and by the time we left for the cruise, I was excited.

This would be our first vacation as a family, and I was determined to enjoy it. We had been planning and saving for it for a long while, and I was just excited to be able to get this time as a family. For this weekend, all I wanted to do was focus on Rob and Cade.

We left that Thursday, scheduled to return the coming Sunday. Those four days were everything I'd hoped they would be. Free from material distractions, we were able to grow together as a family. Without his friends there to divide his loyalties, Rob became the man I'd always dreamed of, the father I'd hoped for my son. At the time, I didn't look too deeply into it, I just accepted it. It's my nature. When things were good, I didn't dwell too deeply on the bad, I just soaked it all in.

That's not to say that things were bad before the trip. In fact, Rob and I had been doing well as a family, and that helped lay the groundwork for such a perfect vacation.

We returned home refreshed, our ties as a family strengthened. This, along with the events of the past few years, would begin to form the foundation for what would be a long road for all of us.

The Disney cruise was in June of 2006. In December of that same year, once again we reached a turning point.

After our vacation, we kept trying for another baby, but there was nothing. I was left with only a dwindling hope, one that continued to fade with each passing month. I still had that dream of a family, but it was one that I feared I would never see.

My doctor gave me a tentative diagnosis of Polycystic Ovary Syndrome, which would explain my infertility. On day 3 of my cycle, I was scheduled to get blood work to confirm the diagnosis.

I was relieved, thinking only that it was a treatable problem. I would get the blood work, which would confirm it, and then I would get medicine to correct the problem. Simple as that, I would be able to have another child.

Day 3 never came.

Acting on suspicion, I took a test. Sure enough, two lines appeared on the test strip. I was a nervous wreck. The last pregnancy had ended so horribly. Even before that, there was Cade- he was so sick the first two years, and the pregnancy itself had so many complications. I just knew something would go wrong.

The reality turned out to be anti-climactic. Contrary to my expectations, God blessed me with a perfectly healthy pregnancy. It was completely uneventful, which should be understood as completely boring!

Around the same time I found out about my pregnancy, our friends and neighbors gave us the news: they were moving to Virginia, where they originally moved from. Sebby had been called to pastor a church there- a whole 10-hour-drive away!

The 670 miles between us was a huge gap. I couldn't imagine what we would do without them! I was sad to see them leave- you could probably even say that I was a little mad about it! In the short time that we had known them, Sebby and Stacy had become a cornerstone in our lives. This would only set the foundation for an even greater friendship that was soon to come.

Bryan and Christina moved into the house that Sebby and his wife vacated. Bryan was Sebby's son; we had met the couple only once before, at a dinner with the family. I had only met them that once, but I knew things would never be the same next door. This new couple was super quiet, definitely not our type.

It wasn't long before things changed. Their daughter's birthday was in January, just a short time after they moved in. By this point, we were already best friends. Somehow, despite our initial differences, we had managed to hit it off. Now we were having dinner together most nights, watching all of our favorite shows together, and of course, the ever-present pot of coffee. They have since moved, following their parents to Virginia, but even to this day, we still enjoy getting together over coffee when we can. Many tears have been shed across those miles, and even today, we miss them so much!

In July of 2007, we welcomed the newest addition into our family: SaraGrace Vaughn. This little redhead quickly became the delight of our lives, brightening up the day with her ready smile, or giving us a laugh with her even quicker pout. She somehow managed to pull off being a tomboy princess, going out "hun-tin" one day wearing camo pants, boots, and carrying a gun, and then following it up the next day sporting a Disney princess dress and crown.

She is my mini-me, and she keeps us on our toes! She is nicknamed Sassy Pants, and for good reason. They say redheads are feisty, and judging by our Gracie's personality, there is a lot of truth to that statement. By this time, the friendship between the Volpes and the Vaughns had cemented into a lifelong relationship. In later times, this friendship would become a rock that would ground us, holding us in the midst of every storm that passed by. Their wise and godly counsel helped to strengthen mine and Rob's marriage and our own spiritual development. Along with the close counsel of my own parents, it was to them that we looked to for advice and wisdom.

I had no idea how much I would need both in the days ahead.

Chapter Six

A LIFE-CHANGING
EXPERIENCE

Nicaragua! Just a few short weeks, and we would be there. I couldn't believe it was really happening.

I stood before the group, nerves stretched taut. Was it the fact of getting up in front of people to talk? Certainly not. I'm an extreme talker by nature. It has been said that I can talk the horns off of a billy goat. I have never met a stranger and have never had any trouble talking to new people.

No, it wasn't the position that made me nervous. It was the subject matter. As a requirement for participating in this mission trip with our church, we had been asked to write out our testimony and prepare to share it at the next meeting.

So now it was here... and what was I to say? I have never had trouble talking with anyone about anything- anything, that is, except for my faith. I'm not sure why that was. I was comfortable with who I was in Jesus, and had been a Christian nearly all of my life. But I never seemed to make my Christianity a topic of conversation. I couldn't begin to process how I was supposed to be able to stand up in front of this group of people with whom I was trying to make friends. I was embarrassed.

Besides that, who would be interested, anyway? My testimony was boring. You know how it is, when someone gets up in church and shares their testimony of how God has brought them out of addiction, abuse, or some terrible situation. Their stories are always so captivating. Mine didn't seem so exciting, by comparison. And who doesn't like a good story? I have always been one for suspense and adventure, and my story had none of that. I had a great life and no one wanted to hear how good I had it. They would think I was just bragging.

Despite all this, here I was, in front of this group of people. I had no choice but to jump in. With a deep breath, I began...

As I shared my story, uneventful as it was, I watched their faces. Would they accept it? Or would they just think that I was just a spoiled brat? But even as I considered my testimony, I began to see it in a different light. I began to see how God had helped me through, even when I didn't realize it. I was so blessed to be raised in a Christian home with both of my parents. The Lord was really good to us. Growing up, I never wanted for anything. I asked Jesus into my heart when I was five years old. Our very large family owned a house on the Suwannee River, and we made many memories there. One weekend, while at the river, I remember telling my Granny that I wanted to ask Jesus into my heart. She led me in prayer and I asked him to be the Lord of my life. Even in these happy times, God was there.

He was there at my marriage to Rob; He was by my side through my troubled pregnancy with Cade and the trials that followed; He was there in the trials of that second pregnancy that ended so suddenly. He was there through my fears with SaraGrace, and even after she was born.

As I shared my testimony, I realized that the "boringness" of my testimony was a testimony in itself. I also realized just how weak my own faith was. I didn't have a great relationship with Christ- I would put Him on a shelf, expecting Him to stay there until I needed Him again. The overwhelming theme of my faith was that I only wanted Jesus when I needed Him. Yet, He wanted me all of the time.

Little did I know that there would come a time when the Lord would become not only an occasional help, but my daily strength.

Why was I here, in Nicaragua? It wasn't my thing, usually. I went to church, but wasn't interested beyond that. I didn't participate much in anything in church that didn't include my wife.

It started with a class that the church offered on Wednesday nights. Normally, I didn't go on Wednesdays, because SaraBeth was in choir. There was no need for me to go to service, so I stayed home.

Then the church announced a new study that they were offering on managing finances. I surprised SaraBeth by insisting that I wanted to go, and so that was what I did while she was in choir. I felt like it was a step in the right direction. What would it hurt to go?

It was around that same time that they announced the Nicaragua trip. I came home from the class that night and spread the worksheets on the table.

"We are going to Nicaragua," I told her. I can only guess what she must have been thinking at hearing this. Later, she told me that she had been praying for this very thing. She wanted a man who would be the leader of our household.

Her first objection to the trip was money. "It's over $1,000 per person to go! We'll never afford it!"

Without hesitation, I said, "Cancel the Disney cruise. Just cancel it."

Her eyes went wide, but she did like I said. We had planned to go on a Disney cruise, the four of us as a family. She called the company and canceled it, and we used the refund to pay for the mission trip, along with the help of my wife's parents.

We packed for the trip and told our kids goodbye. They were too young to go, and would be staying with Gamma and Papa for the week.

So now here we were- and "here" is where I would be faced with myself. This is where I met "me."

I saw things on this trip that I never even knew before. People who had cardboard homes, people who had to walk miles just to get some water. These were the people that we were working with.

We went out visiting every day. We met with the people in the area, getting to know them and sharing about God. We would split up. Some would go to the schools and do a fiesta, while the rest went door to door. It was so different from anything in America. The people were excited that Americans would actually want to come visit them. They were very kind.

On the third day of the trip, it was our turn to go out visiting. This would take anywhere from 45 minutes to a few hours. It just depended on how many people were in that house.

We walked up to a house that had a mother and two kids. The mother and her daughter were sweeping the dirt floor of their home. The boy was outside working in the yard. I walked over to him and started talking to him.

I was amazed at what he told me. I learned that he had to finish the work around the house before he went to school. He said most days, he couldn't go because he had so much to do, but he liked going to school because he liked to learn.

Like most people, my first thought was of all the kids in the U.S. that hate school. They would do anything to get out of going, and yet, here is a kid that would love to go to school but can't.

What he said next was even more eye-opening, and it hit me like a ton of bricks. The boy said he had to stay home because his dad left them, and he was the only male to work. He hated his father for leaving them, and he said he had anger problems because of this.

It was like I was talking to myself. I had the same problem. I felt anger because I didn't understand why my father didn't want anything to do with me. So I had problems with everything in my life. I just didn't see it before now. So what do you say to a kid with the same problems as you?

At this very moment, I found who and what Jesus Christ was about! It was like I was talking and being talked to at the same time.

Then I said something I would never have said before.

"You have to forgive him because if you don't, you can't move forward."

It wasn't me talking now. I wasn't only talking to this kid, I was talking to me- and it was Christ talking to me. It was His words, and it was driving home for me. I said, "Jesus forgives us, so we need to forgive others."

It's hard to hear that because we hold on to so much hurt sometimes, but it's true that to forgive is not in man's nature. We hold on to every little thing someone does to us. Someone can do something nice for you, and you forget about it in a few weeks or a month later. But if someone did something to you that you hate, you remember it forever. It's almost like you're saying, "I will never let that happen again," but Christ says to forgive. Why?

Because forgiveness isn't of this world.

I learned a lot in that moment. Later that night, I prayed that Christ Jesus would come in my life and let His Spirit change me and make me a different person, a person to serve Him, a person to make a difference. I didn't care what I did. I just knew I was hooked on the Gospel of Jesus Christ.

I came home from that trip a changed man. I stopped drinking and partying and started focusing on family. Some people say you can't stop drinking overnight, but I am here to say that "You can do all things through Christ." I didn't go to any meeting or anything like that. I just stopped.

That is Christ Jesus right there. Not me. I couldn't have done that.

We as a family started getting involved in church and started growing more in Christ. We were already close to our neighbors, Bryan and Christina. But now, the relationship took on new meaning. Bryan is my best friend today and he has played a huge part in my growth as a Christian. I think every person should have a Bryan in their life.

A year or so later, Bryan told me he was being called back to Virginia to pastor a church. I couldn't argue with that because if he wouldn't have listened the first time God told him to move, I would have never met him. Still, it was hard to see my best friend move away, because we talked all the time.

The years passed and our family had problems just like every person in the world has. God moved us to another church and my wife became pregnant again. But this pregnancy would change everything in my life and the life of my family forever.

Chapter Seven

PREGNANT AGAIN

Nearly a year after our Nicaragua trip, I started writing a blog. At first, it was only as a way to keep in touch with family and friends, especially those who were long-distance. We still missed the Volpes, both senior and younger, and we kept in regular contact with them. With this blog, I could keep them updated all at once with what was going on in our lives.

I had no idea how much this tiny thread of communication would become a lifeline for me, a platform on which I could pour out my heart. Eventually, it would become more than just family and friends-strangers I had never met would stumble across my blog, becoming caught up in my story.

As time went on, especially during Faith's pregnancy, it was like a soothing river just running through the rocks in our life. I met many people that became instant friends (some I've never seen in person), and so many people would leave us such encouraging comments. It was a tangible tool that God used to show us Faith's life was going to make a difference.

On April 29, 2009, I wrote my first post:

Well, I finally made it to the blog world. I have held off as long as possible, but I just gave in. God has put it on my heart for some time to do this, so I hope it will glorify Him. Of course it will be filled with stories and pics of our precious children, but I hope it will be an encouragement to those who read it.

I titled the blog, "More Than Enough." To me, it was fitting. Toward the end of the first post, I wrote these words, illustrating what the title meant to me:

The many friendships in my life, that mean so much to me.... are More Than Enough to love and support me.

The great (most days) job that I have in this terrible economy.... is More Than Enough to meet our needs.

My most wonderful family that I am so close to... is More Than Enough to count on anytime I need them.

My more than AMAZING husband, whom I love unconditionally, who is a changed man following God's desires for his heart... is way More Than Enough to love me for who I am.

My most PRECIOUS miracles, Cade and SaraGrace, who were never to be mine, but God was more powerful than any doctor or treatment... are More Than Enough for me to love and cherish every second I have with them. They make me a better Mama.

And the GREATEST gift of all, my SALVATION... is More Than Enough to see me through this earthly life, and to escort me to see my Savior when I get to heaven.

The blog started out as just the occasional post about my family, what was going on in our lives. I posted about trips, weddings, and the small moments. Occasionally, I posted what was on my heart, spilling out my thoughts on God, relationships, and the price of living in a fallen world.

It was a typical cutesy kind of blog, meant to update friends and family and to share what was on my heart and mind.

And then it became more.

For the first year after I started the blog, nothing really happened. My posts ran the same thread as countless other blogs out there. I updated a few times every month, despite a firm resolution to update more often. We went on another mission trip to Costa Rica. Cade started kindergarten, and then first grade. He joined tackle football after waiting six years to be able to take someone out and not get in trouble. For her second birthday, SaraGrace enjoyed her birthday cake that I'd made especially for her, the one with Princess Ariel.

Birthday cakes, a new puppy, Halloween costumes, and both the joys and tears of another year passing- these are the posts that filled my blog in that first year. Rob and I were both growing in the Lord and in our relationship. We were even discussing the possibility of being missionaries! Two years ago, it was a possibility I could never have dreamed of, but God does work in amazing ways!

Life continued as normal. Then in late 2010, I became pregnant. From the beginning, I was tense. Between Cade's problems, the ectopic pregnancy, and my own misshapen uterus, the odds were against me. Sure, SaraGrace had turned out fine, with no complications for either of us- but who was to say I'd get that lucky a second time?

Shortly after starting my own blog, I stumbled across several others, which I began to follow religiously. I found them quite by accident, but they struck a chord in my heart nonetheless. It first came about while I was searching for a song by the Christian group Selah. Rob and I were wanting to do a special for our church, called "Precious Lord, Take My Hand."

An Internet search for this song pulled up a blog hosted by a wonderful lady, Angie Smith. Her husband is the lead singer for Selah. I read her story of how they'd received a fatal diagnosis at her 20-week ultrasound. How they carried the baby to term, despite doctor recommendations. How finally, the baby was born, only to die within two hours of birth. She'd blogged the entire time and had generated a huge following from it.

The story stuck with me, along with countless others I found. It struck home the sad reality that the more times you got pregnant, the greater the odds of having complications.

And here I was- pregnant. With my third child. My fourth pregnancy.

Rob gave me a hard time about it. He couldn't see why I wanted to read all that sad stuff all the time. I would read these stories and just sit there and cry.

Now, I couldn't shake the feeling that something was wrong. They often say that the first indication that something is wrong is the mother's instinct, right? I don't know if I could stand to lose another baby.

I wrote,

> I will have to be honest. I have been extremely worried. I suffered an ectopic pregnancy before SaraGrace, and for some reason could not shake the fact that something is going to happen this time. I have cried, lost sleep, and prayed and prayed and prayed, like 4 to 5 times an hour.

Finally, I stopped worrying long enough to listen to what my Heavenly Father had to say.

"SaraBeth, if you're not trusting me, you're trusting someone or something. Are you really going to trust Satan over me?"

That struck me hard. I didn't know what His plan was for this baby, but God did. He knew how the story would end. I knew then that God was in control, and I had to trust Him completely with this child, as I had with the others.

A week after the pregnancy test, I had my first ultrasound. To my amazement, everything looked great, and we were even able to hear a tiny heartbeat!

I happily reported the news on my blog, rejoicing that, "God is so good!"

Chapter Eight

THREATENED

The word "threatened" is mostly associated with the feeling of fear. If someone threatens you, it is typically out of anger. If you feel threatened by someone or something, it brings anxiety. I cannot think of any positive way in which the word "threatened" could be used.

I have heard the word used many times in my 34 years, but never before had it bothered me the way it did on that Monday.

It was 11 days after my first ultrasound. I had been spotting, and they just wanted to check things out. This time, it took the technician a while to find the baby. Finally, there was a heartbeat. I was amazed as I watched that steady beat, knowing that it came from my own baby.

I was equally frightened- what if something was wrong? They say that the first sign of problem is often the mother's instinct. My mind flashed back to my worry of two weeks ago, and I felt my heart begin to sink.

I watched the technician anxiously as she came to a final conclusion. The baby hadn't grown like it should have. In addition, I had a blood clot in my uterus. All these findings came to one diagnosis: "threatened miscarriage."

I was heartbroken. Those are not the words you ever want to hear. A mother never wants to hear that her child is "threatened" in any way, whether they are already here on earth, or waiting in the womb.

I was scheduled for a follow-up appointment a week later. It was a tough week, but one that grew me in my faith in God. A week that taught me that there are some things in life I can't control. One that taught me that no matter what, His plan is perfect!

I can't say I was perfectly at peace or that my worries had completely gone away, but I was learning to trust in God.

Amy went with me to the appointment. She has been my very best friend for years. We have been through *everything* together. Joys, heartaches, losses; you name it, we've done it. I was so glad that she offered to go with me. I was a bit nervous when we walked in, because I was just ready to know what was going on.

The ultrasound technician started the scan, and it was a breathless few minutes while she completed the procedure. She was looking for the blood clot reported at the last appointment, but to her surprise, there was nothing! She couldn't believe it, but I could. I knew it had to be God.

It was the first of what would become many times when God showed up and showed out. I had never seen an answered prayer like this before. We had so many people praying for us, and I just knew that it had to be the power of prayer. I cried, joy and relief mingling together.

I was at peace. God was in control.

Chapter Nine

TROUBLED

Monday, November 1st, 2010, I had another follow-up ultrasound just to give us peace of mind that everything was as it should be. We soon found out it was not. That day, we saw a very different baby on the tiny black and white screen. The baby's heart rate was high, too high, which struck a chord of concern. It also appeared that our baby was suffering from gastroschisis- a birth defect in which the intestines are growing outside of the body.

I was upset to say the least, but my doctor reassured me that if this was indeed what we were dealing with, it was fixable. I was transferred to the care of a perinatologist and scheduled for a Level 2 ultrasound to give us a definite diagnosis.

Amy is hardheaded and stubborn. Before the appointment, I felt fine, confident enough to go on my own. Nothing was wrong, so why worry? After all, the last appointment had shown that everything was clear. Still, she insisted on going. It's moments like these that make us such close friends. My own stubbornness is only equal to hers, so I knew I had met my match.

God gives us the most awesome blessings in the midst of our trials. She originally had plans to go see the space shuttle that day, but the launch had been canceled due to the weather. She called me that morning and asked if I needed her to go with me. She had already done so much, and I thought I would be fine. Now, I was glad for her stubbornness, because I knew I needed a friend beside me as I received the doctor's news. God had gone before me and worked out the smallest detail so that I didn't have to hear this news alone. Thankfully, He provides even when we do not think we need provision.

Obviously, this news changed everything about my pregnancy- my doctor, my hospital, the care of my baby. I was scared, but I realized that Jesus walked this road before me, so He knew how I felt.

That didn't make it any less difficult, however. Amy and I walked out to the parking lot, where she did her best to comfort me. We both shed tears that day. Through her tears, she told me that it was going to be okay. I don't know what I would have done without her that day, or in the days ahead. For that matter, I don't know what I would have done without the firm support of my own family, as well.

When we finally left, I drove off with tears streaming down my face. I couldn't see the lines on the interstate. I couldn't even see the road signs through my tears. I don't know how I made it back to work, but somehow I managed it.

I called my mom to tell her the news, but I couldn't even talk. I felt like the wind had been sucked out of me. I had already called to tell Rob, but since I could hardly speak, that conversation didn't last long.

At first, my mother could hardly understand me. She instantly went into Mommy mode, telling me to slow down and take a deep breath. She kept assuring me that it would be alright, and to trust God.

Because she wasn't there at the ultrasound, she didn't yet understand the ramifications of the diagnosis. How could she? I could barely understand it myself.

My first instinct was to pray selfishly that nothing would be wrong, that this baby would be perfect. But then I realized- "this is not my baby, not my story." I had made the decision in the beginning to give this baby to God. This was His story to write and tell.

Rob and I decided, right then and there, to be grateful that God had chosen us to tell His story and to share all that He had done and was going to do. Was it going to be an easy road? Absolutely not! No parent wants to hear that their child is not "normal." But we were not on this journey alone. Just as God was with Shadrach, Meshach, and Abednego in the fiery furnace, and just as He was with Daniel in the lion's den, He would be with us as we navigated the road ahead.

Monday, November 15, 2010 is a day that changed our lives forever. It was our first appointment and ultrasound with the perinatologist. As I anticipated the afternoon's appointment, it couldn't come fast enough.

As we walked through the doors of the new clinic, I was overcome with two completely different emotions. On the one hand, God had granted me a peace that He was in control. On the other hand, the Mama in me was begging to kick in and I was scared out of my mind. What if something was wrong? We signed in and waited for our turn.

Before the appointment, I sent out a prayer request to my blog readers:

> *Today is a big day for us. We have our first appointment with the perinatologist this afternoon. Of course, it can't come fast enough, but I am thankful for the peace that I know has come from only God. Please pray for us today as we will begin this journey into the unknown. Please pray specifically that they will be able to give us a definite diagnosis, as the waiting is the hardest part!*
>
> *I will update tomorrow with the answers we get. Thank you to each of you that has covered us and our baby in your prayers. We have definitely felt them.*

We walked into that appointment, nervous but little more. I was only thinking of how to care for a baby with special needs, of how we would handle NICU.

The doctor's demeanor didn't settle my skipping heart at all. He was all business, clicking away on the monitor without a word. I told Rob that something was wrong, but he insisted I was reading too much into it. The man was just doing his job.

It was amazing to see all of the details on the Level 2 ultrasound. The baby seemed so happy, moving and kicking all over the place. He was bouncing throughout the entire ultrasound. It couldn't be all that bad.

After spending a few minutes alone to read the results, the doctor returned and invited us back to his office. We slowly walked down the tiny hallway and sat down in a very small office. The office felt old and sad. It had a wooden table in the middle of the tiny room.

As we walked in, the doctor laid the pictures down on the table for us to see. My heart stopped in that moment. Something was wrong.

I was bracing myself for the worst. At the same time, I just prayed that it was fixable.

Before getting into the diagnosis, he gave us some great news: we were going to have a boy!

Mack... that was to be our baby's name. Rob and I had long discussed it, that if we were to have another boy, it would be "Mack." He was to be named after Rob's stepdad, who in his heart was his real dad. It was a moment that meant a lot to us. To hear that I was having a boy, it was a ray of sunshine in a very rainy day.

Then the doctor proceeded with his findings. The diagnosis was grim. My heart dropped as he explained it to us.

Amniotic Band Syndrome. That was the diagnosis.

Amniotic Band Syndrome is when the inner amniotic membrane ruptures at some point, and in an effort to fuse back together, they constrict and pull, which ultimately had left all the organs exposed, including the heart and lungs. There is no treatment option.

"It isn't good. It isn't good at all."

As he laid out the diagnosis before us, the doctor presented us with the only option he felt was available.

Termination. Abort the pregnancy.

Chapter Ten

PROGNOSIS

There was no way we could consider abortion. I never thought it would be something I would be faced with. So many times we associate those who have chosen abortion with a certain socio-economic status. I didn't fit any of those. But my perspective would soon change.

The doctor said that he didn't believe the baby would survive in utero, but we had to believe that our Heavenly Father would take the baby when He was ready. After all, we had already been faced with a threatened miscarriage, and God chose to allow him to stay with us.

The doctor informed us that we were continuing with this pregnancy against his better judgment. We were told that if we indeed made it to full term, the doctors and hospital would do nothing for our child, since there really was nothing they could do. Armed with that information, we requested to remain under the care of our regular obstetrician and deliver at the hospital that we loved so much.

As we walked out of the office and headed to the elevator, we didn't say a word to each other. I held tightly to those ultrasound pictures as if my baby's life depended on it. I was a crying wreck, and Rob was just silent.

We got in the elevator with several other pregnant women. I couldn't help but notice the smiling mothers surrounding me while my world was crumbling apart.

As we got off on our floor, Rob headed for the bathroom. I stood in the hall, leaning against the wall for support, and buried my face in my hands, letting the tears come. A sweet stranger walked up to me and put her hand on my shoulder.

"I don't know what you are going through, but can I pray for you?"

Wow! That lady had some courage. I realized then what a testimony we could be to others. We could choose from this point on to be bitter and mad at God, or we could choose to allow Him to use the life of our child to bring Him glory and share His love with so many others.

As Rob walked out of the restroom, I could see his face stained with tears. His eyes were red and puffy, but he was determined to hold it together for me.

The appointment was fairly short, though it seemed like an eternity. We got back to the car and hashed out what had just happened. We called my mother, who had been anxiously waiting to hear the treatment options. She couldn't understand what I was telling her because I was so upset. We went over to their house for dinner that night.

When everything is falling apart, my Mom and Dad are my rock. They are the ones who have held me up and held me accountable. They have taught me to always do what is right, regardless of how hard it may be. From them, I learned that God will always bless the decision to do the right thing- even in a situation such as this.

When I look at my testimony, I have to thank God for giving me godly parents, who worked to stay married, provide a Christian home, and give us a great moral understanding. They had raised us in the knowledge of the Bible, that God knows each of us, even my child who had been deemed "not compatible with life." We were all important to Him, and He has plans for all of us. They are the epitome of selfless love. I am so thankful to them for their examples of marriage, parenting, and being a Christian.

When the hard times came, I knew who to look to for support and counsel. So it was now. We went over for dinner because I knew that I needed my mother's strength, my father's wisdom.

My sister, nine months pregnant at the time, was also joining us for dinner. She walked in the front door and saw us all in tears. After hearing the news, she was devastated, even as she felt a surge of guilt at the health of her own baby.

I think it was then that I realized that this would be a hard road for all of us. However, we held on to the fact that God's plan is always perfect. We knew that He had a purpose for our baby and that the next few weeks would be tough. But we also knew the love of our Savior would sustain us. We decided to carry our little child until God saw fit to take him home.

We had claimed Jeremiah 29:11 as the verse for this baby's life: "For I know the plans I have for you, declares the Lord. Plans to prosper you, not to harm you. Plans to give you hope and a future" (NIV). We had to trust in the promise of that verse, in what it meant for us. The news was horrible, but God had good plans in store for us, and He knew it better than we did.

That same day, I called my primary doctor, Dr. Bartram. Of course, she offered to continue to oversee our care. We scheduled an appointment for Wednesday so we could discuss my care as we moved forward.

Dr. Bartram had been a part of my life for several years. I was transferred to her practice when I became pregnant again after Cade-the ectopic pregnancy. I had never met her before the day she had to tell me I was going to lose my second child.

She was so kind and compassionate, and I respected her so much. Several months later, when I became pregnant once again, I loved having her as my doctor. She delivered SaraGrace and I couldn't imagine having a baby without her there for the delivery. I couldn't wait to sit down and discuss our baby with her.

Rob and I sat face to face with the doctor in an exam room. She looked at me, held both of my hands, and listened to all we had to say. She cried with me as I struggled to get the words out.

I had a sheet of yellow legal paper with a list of questions I needed to have answered. As my doctor, she had to give me all the medical options. She knew this would be a hard journey for us, and suggested I have a DNC. The doctor was worried for me and all I would have to endure by carrying a baby we knew would probably not survive.

A DNC is a surgical procedure where they dilate the cervix and scrape out the uterus. Usually, it is performed after a miscarriage, to make sure that all the fetal tissue is removed.

It's used for a miscarriage. I was still carrying my baby- a baby that was very much alive. It would be an abortion.

I couldn't bear the thought of my baby ending up in a trash can or a biohazard bin somewhere. He was more than that to me. He wasn't some phantom fetus; he was our son.

The doctor then mentioned that our baby may be experiencing pain. Hearing this, I began to question if we were doing the right thing. Were we just being selfish?

I knew that God had called us to this journey, but I already felt so sorry for my child and I couldn't imagine intentionally allowing him to suffer. Seeing my indecision, the doctor told us to call her the next day and let her know what we had decided.

We left there confused and angry. How could everyone be so quick to do away with our child? But then, how could we go on knowing we were causing him pain?

This is when my perspective on abortion changed. For so many years, I couldn't understand how people could just *kill* innocent babies. But the medical profession makes it sound so easy, and they want you to believe it will be over in a second. We had two doctors begging us to terminate our child. Even we ourselves questioned if we were doing the right thing by keeping this baby. I now understand why women can feel like it will all go away once the choice is made. Sadly, that is not true.

We just didn't know what to do. We knew in our hearts that God gave this baby to us for a reason. But as parents, we couldn't bear the thought of making a decision that would prolong the pain for our child.

We called our friend, Bryan, for some counsel. He and his wife's spiritual mentoring had been invaluable to us over the years. I don't know how we would have made it through the last several years without them.

Bryan knew our hearts and knew that we just needed reassurance. He encouraged us that we were doing the right thing, but he also said that we needed to pray about it. We then called our own pastor, Pastor Calvin Carr. Pastor Calvin offered to meet with us immediately.

At the meeting, we shared with him our desire to be obedient to God's calling and carry our child, though we knew it wouldn't be easy. When we told him about the possibility of him being in pain, he said something that will stick with me forever.

"If you are going to trust God with your baby, then you need to trust Him to provide comfort for the baby."

Why didn't I think of that? I then knew we were doing exactly what we were called to do, and I called my doctor to share with her our decision.

We were going to keep this baby.

Chapter Eleven

UPDATES

Friday, November 19, 2010 - Thankful

It has been only 4 days since we got the news of our baby. It seems like an eternity! But we are clinging to Jesus and all the things we have to be thankful for.

First and foremost, we are thankful for our relationship with Jesus. It amazes us that just when you think you can't go another day, He gives us the grace to make it through. I can't imagine how anyone could make it through such a time as this, without the hope that Jesus gives!

We are thankful for each other. Rob and I have faced many trials in our married life. And as hard as some of those were, we are thankful that God has used them to strengthen our relationship. I can't imagine going through any of this with anyone else.

We are thankful for our 2 children at home, Cade and SaraGrace. We now look at them so differently, and realize all of the things we have taken for granted in being their parents. Cade is absolutely devastated and has tons of questions, but he kisses his baby all the time and tells him how much he loves him, and that he'll always be his big brother. Boy what we can learn from our children.

We are thankful for our families. What a blessing to have everyone so near to us. They have been our rock.

We are thankful for friends, near and far. We have been overwhelmed by the love and support from friends, and God has blessed us with so many. Thank you to everyone who calls, writes, or comments, even when you don't have the words. We don't have the words either, but you have been such an encouragement to us!

We are thankful for our little boy, Mack Andrew. His life is touching people already, and it's only just begun. We are thankful for what we are learning through him. He has changed our lives tremendously in his 12 weeks of life. We are thankful for every day we are blessed with his presence. And most of all, we are thankful that God has chosen US to be his parents!

Friday, December 3, 2010 – Ecstatic

I have the cutest pictures to share with you from Thanksgiving, but they will have to wait until I can find that pesky little cord that keeps walking away.

But I did want to share that I felt Baby Mack move for the first time yesterday. I'm so thankful for that blessing! It made my day!!!

Wednesday, December 8, 2010 - Yesterday

Yesterday was a tough day. I have had a really good two weeks, and have been overwhelmed with peace and strength, but yesterday was a breakdown.

We had an ultrasound appointment. I wanted so badly to include our baby on our Christmas cards this year, so they scheduled another ultrasound. Amy, our ultrasound tech, is AMAZING! She has photographed our baby from the very beginning, at just 6 weeks. She has been so kind and loving, and I am just so thankful for her.

Of course, I had my BFF Amy with me, and my mom came this time too. It was the first time she has gotten to see the baby in action.

When Amy [the technician] got started, I could tell that our sweet baby had grown, which also means that you could see all that is going on. That was harder than I expected. The heart is still beating strongly. We watched the baby put its hand to its face. It really was AMAZING!

I asked Amy to confirm that it really was a Mack. Guess what! It's a GIRL! So Mack is now Faith Mackenzie Vaughn. Rob picked out the name Faith, because that is the only thing that keeps us going.

I cherish each time we get to see our baby, but I won't lie. It gets harder and harder. As a Mama, it's hard to see your child have all of these problems that no one can fix. I just want to take her out, hold her, tell her how much I love her, and that it's all going to be ok. I want to tell her that Jesus is going to take such good care of her.

I find myself in a place between having faith in God that He can heal our baby girl, and also having faith in God that even if it is not His plan that our child be healed, He is the same as He was before this child came to be. I know that He is the Great Physician, and that He could heal her in an instant. But I also know that His plan may be different than my plan for our child. And if it is, it doesn't mean He loves us or our daughter any less. In fact, He has confidence in us that we can tell His story.

Some days can be so crippling. But I don't want to be crippled. I have never in my life wanted so badly to tell people about Jesus than I do now. I also want to tell people all about our daughter; how she has changed our lives; how He has changed our lives. I pray every day that Jesus will use me to bring glory to Him, and that He will give me what I need to point people to Him.

It wasn't Mack Andrew, after all. We got it wrong. My wife had her appointment, where they had another ultrasound. Instead of the boy we were expecting, there was a surprise. They told her that the baby was actually a girl.

We had to come up with a different name, but I already knew what I wanted it to be. Faith Mackenzie Vaughn. "Mackenzie" to keep the "Mack" name. And Faith... "Faith," because we were going to need a lot of faith to get through this. Faith would be the only thing to keep us going.

There is nothing more difficult as a father than to watch your children suffer. I could do nothing other than to watch while doctors made decisions about my family that had nothing to do with me. They wanted us to abort the baby. Their words were so simple, so sure. We could abort the baby, and it would be okay, because it would be over in a few days and we could get pregnant again soon. They would even do it today.

I couldn't think about throwing this away so easily. This was my baby, my little girl. What kind of father would I be if I let her go that quickly?

Fathers fight for their children. I would fight for mine if I had the chance. But they said there was no chance. How do you fight for someone who doesn't have a chance?

So I couldn't fight. I just had to pray, and see what God had for us. I knew there had to be a reason He gave us this baby. I gave it to God. If the baby lived, it was because of God. If the baby passed away it would be God's decision, not my decision.

Sometimes we take the easy road because it's too hard, but Jesus said being a Christian would not be easy, and we need to put our faith to the test.

This would be the biggest test of our lives.

Chapter Twelve

A Heavy Heart

I blogged throughout my entire pregnancy and the events following. I didn't want to forget any of it. I wanted to keep it as it was then, fresh and raw. I knew that there would come a day, as they got older, that SaraGrace and Cade would begin to ask questions, and I wanted to have the answers ready for them.

Even now, they were already having a hard time with it. It was just after the New Year. We'd gotten the ultrasound pictures for our Christmas card, and they were proud of their baby sister. SaraGrace was just beginning to comprehend what was going on. As a Mama, it was so hard to see her struggle, knowing there wasn't much I could do for her.

Cade handled it differently, internalizing everything. When we finally sat him down to talk about it, the first thing that came out was his anger. He was mad that his sister had to die. We couldn't do anything but just pray that God would direct and guide us in what to say to him.

At the same time, there was sweetness to counter his anger. We were planning on taking a family vacation in the near future, and in the midst of this conversation, Cade jumped in. "Mommy, every year on Faith's birthday, can we go do something fun to remember her?"

That just melted my heart! The openness of his heart was a sweet flavor in the middle of all the bitter news.

Later, during choir practice at church, our song director shared how we sometimes become so self-contained, that we do not feel like we have to rely on God for anything. But then things come along, and we find that we have nothing else but Him, that we have to cry out to Him. Jesus loves it when we cry out to Him and give Him all of our burdens.

As I thought on this truth, I posted this on my blog:

> *I just want to encourage you to give EVERYTHING to Jesus. Not just your blessings and your thanks, but your burdens as well. Let Him bless you with the peace that passes all understanding. I am so thankful for all of the ways we have been able to see God at work-especially in the small details. He cares so much about the little details that you have to know He cares about the big things too. I probably would be missing out on those things, if it weren't for Faith. I just find myself falling more in love with Him, and longing for even more of a relationship.*
>
> *It amazes me that He knows my name, my every thought, and as the songs says, He sees each tear that falls, and hears me when I call.*
>
> *Please pray for us over the next few weeks, as we seek God's will in the details of our Faith. We want Him to get the glory for all of the great things He has and will do!*

Psalm 40: 1-3

¹ I waited patiently for the Lord; and he inclined unto me, and heard my cry.

² He brought me up also out of an horrible pit, out of the miry clay, and set my feet upon a rock, and established my goings.

³ And he hath put a new song in my mouth, even praise unto our God: many shall see it, and fear, and shall trust in the Lord.

The date was January 13th, 2011. Our goal for this month was to have all of the arrangements for Faith put together. We were still hoping and praying for a miracle, but if it wasn't God's plan, we wanted to be as prepared as possible.

There is nothing more heartbreaking than having to prepare the funeral arrangements for your own unborn child. We should be preparing the nursery for her arrival, planning for a wonderful addition to our family. It was to be a joyous time, one of anticipation, going through all the questions that any new parents have. Who would she look like most? When would she cross her first milestones? Her first laugh, her first steps? What would be her first word? Daddy's girl or Mommy's girl? What color would her eyes be?

Would she even open her eyes on this earth? Every day that passed, our hearts grew heavy with the weight of her diagnosis. We hoped for a miracle, but braced for the worst. Would she even make it to full term?

Chapter Thirteen

MAKING ARRANGEMENTS

Our next appointment was set for Tuesday, January 18. Dr. Bartram ran the Doppler to check her heart rate and checked everything else. Faith had a good, strong heartbeat, which was encouraging to hear.

We also tentatively set the date for the C-section: May 11th, 2011. It was surreal to know the date your own daughter would be born, and when she would most likely die.

Following the appointment, we met with the funeral home to take care of the arrangements. I had dreaded this day since November 15th, but knew we needed to be prepared in the event our Faith was called to heaven.

Rob and I were overwhelmed with the details, but also the cost. Funerals aren't cheap. I prayed before we went in there that God would just show up, lift us up, and give us the strength to get through it.

We have known the owners of Milam Funeral Home for many years. They have long been friends of the family. When Ashley came out to discuss with us the details of the funeral arrangements, she told us that they would be waiving all of their fees. As a policy, they don't charge for funerals for children under two years old.

We would only be responsible for minimal costs, such as the casket and obituary.

Praise God! What a blessing. Even in the middle of a tragedy, God is still there. It was as if He said to us, "Hang on! I'm right here. I have it all under control."

We went ahead and picked out the casket. It was a simple white one, with only a few embellishments. I thought it was very fitting for our beautiful little girl.

We got a lot of flak for making all these preparations. People said we didn't have enough faith, that we weren't trusting God to heal her. On the contrary, we never assumed she would not be healed- but we never assumed that she would definitely be healed, either. We did know that God doesn't always work like we would want Him to. *Could* He heal her? Certainly- but it doesn't mean that it was His plan.

The funeral arrangements were our plan B. Not knowing God's plan or what the future held for us, we needed to be ready. Maybe His plan wasn't to heal her- maybe it was to show His love and grace in a time of great trial.

In the event that she did pass away, we didn't want to have to be bogged down with the details. I needed to be a Mommy to my other two children, to be ready to provide them the comfort they would need. The last thing I needed was to be focused on last-minute preparations.

The very next day, we had another ultrasound appointment, just to see how the baby was doing. I picked up Amy and we went ahead to the doctor's office.

The last appointment had been very hard. Our baby had grown, which also meant that you could see even more clearly her disfigurement. On the last ultrasound, our sweet baby was folded nearly in half from the scoliosis, a side effect of her diagnosis. Hers was a severe case.

I was beside myself. I wanted so badly for my kids to be a part of her life, to be able to hold their baby sister. I didn't want them to be scared, or to have horrific memories of their disfigured sister.

Now, as they prepped me for the ultrasound, I was prepared for the worst. If it was so bad last time, how much worse would it be now?

The little black and white screen came to life, and Faith's little face appeared. As her body came into view, I gasped, tears beginning to stream down my cheeks.

Her little body had straightened out! Her legs and feet were where they were supposed to be, and were kicking wildly on the screen.

I sent up a breathless prayer of thanks, thanking God right then and there for being there with me. I just laid there, in awe of what He was doing to her little body. Was He fixing everything and making it all okay? No, not at the time- but He was doing just enough to baffle us all and to let us know that only HE was in control of little Faith.

Faith's diagnosis remained the same, but there was some encouragement in that ultrasound. She had shown some improvement in her growth milestones. Her stomach and bladder appeared to be normal this time, a far different picture from the last appointment. I was able to get a 4D picture of her face, and she looked just like SaraGrace.

We still didn't know what our Savior had planned for her, but we were not giving up hope that He would heal her. In just 6 short weeks, our baby looked completely different, and in a great and miraculous way. If it was not His will that she remain on this earth, we knew beyond a shadow of a doubt that He was using her and her story to impact people for Him. What an honor!

Thursday, January 20th, 2011 – God is Good!

I would like to let you know that this Sunday, our church, as well as many others, will be observing Sanctity of Human Life Sunday. This time will be a time to celebrate the miracle of precious life that our Creator has blessed us with. During our journey, we have learned so many statistics, but the one most devastating is the number of babies that are terminated because we do not deem them to be perfect! Did you know that the majority of pregnancies that test positive for Down Syndrome are terminated? That is astounding! I know that our Faith may not be perfect in the eyes of the world, but I know beyond a shadow of a doubt that she is perfect in the eyes of Jesus. She is just who He created her to be.

Psalm 139:13-16

[13] For thou hast possessed my reins: thou hast covered me in my mother's womb.

[14] I will praise thee; for I am fearfully and wonderfully made: marvelous are thy works; and that my soul knoweth right well.

[15] My substance was not hid from thee, when I was made in secret, and curiously wrought in the lowest parts of the earth.

[16] Thine eyes did see my substance, yet being unperfect; and in thy book all my members were written, which in continuance were fashioned, when as yet there was none of them.

But the wonderful thing about God is His unending love, mercy and forgiveness. For those who are living with the regret of decisions made in the past, please know that anything that is laid before Jesus is never unredeemed. Jesus Saves! Jesus Forgives! He can use you and your story to change the lives of others.

Chapter Fourteen
A GROWING GIRL

We had yet another appointment a week later. It was actually supposed to be the next day, but Cade had an accident at school, and we ended up rushing him to the ER with a concussion. He was throwing up and had a major headache, but other than that, he was fine. No injuries, brain or otherwise. It was a great blessing in the midst of a huge trial. In fact, when he got back to school the next day, our first-grader was proud to show off where he'd gotten the "RV" in his arm!

Thursday's appointment was one long delayed. It was back at Shands this time, with the perinatologist.

I didn't ever want to go back to Shands. The doctor wasn't supportive of our decision to carry her; in fact, he made it perfectly clear he wouldn't even attempt to do anything for her. So I was just content in staying with my current doctor at North Florida.

I was first scheduled for an appointment within a month after the first diagnosis, back in November. I canceled it because I'd heard enough bad news about my baby, and I didn't want to be made to feel guilty for keeping her.

But God wouldn't leave me alone about it. Over the next several weeks, the Holy Spirit really laid it on my heart that I needed to go back, even if it was hard. I called to reschedule, but ended up missing that appointment, too, because of Cade's accident.

It still wasn't enough. Still feeling like I needed to go, I again rescheduled. Due to the clinical rotations, we landed with a different doctor, Dr. Duff. I would soon come to see how much my Heavenly Father had worked out all the delays. He cares about the little details, I tell you.

I was apprehensive when we walked in for the appointment. There was that bathroom from last time- the very same one where Rob fell apart. We had just received the news. My heart sank as we passed that fateful room, that place in the hallway where I just sat and cried.

Then there was the waiting room. Everyone else was so happy. As we walked into that doctor's office, it was hard to keep back the tears. Oh, the joy on the faces of the young mothers that sat there, yet Satan was doing everything we could to overcome what little joy we had.

Some people were even rude to the desk clerk. I made the comment that if they only knew how good they had it, they wouldn't be so rude. My husband gave me this piece of wisdom in response: "You have to remember, this is the story God wrote for us, not them."

He was right, of course. We had decided to give it all to God for His glory. I had to let go of the bitterness already beginning to form.

Through it all, it was amazing to see God working even in the little things. Even now, He continued to come through. The technician came out to call us to the back, and I was happily surprised to find a face I recognized. I have known her for years, but I had no idea she worked there!

Mrs. Gail started the ultrasound, and once again I got to see my little one's face. During the ultrasound, Faith was kicking around like a ninja. It was amazing to see her so active! We were able to get some really cute pictures of her face and hands.

She looked much the same as she had the week before, with one major difference: Her heart appeared to have settled in her chest cavity. The week before, it had been on the outside. Now, not only was it in its correct position, it also appeared perfectly healthy, with all four chambers! The doctor informed us that her lungs had also formed, despite a previous thought that they wouldn't be able to form at all. God was good!

In my heart, I felt the consistent urging to confirm whether it was indeed a fatal diagnosis. Dr. Duff wiped my bulging belly after the ultrasound was completed. I watched him closely and asked, "Are we sure that there is nothing that can be done?"

He thought for a moment before giving his answer. I appreciated his thoughtful manner, the way he carefully considered the matter instead of just brushing it aside.

In a thoughtful tone, he explained that the main issue wasn't whether the organs were all there, or that they hadn't developed properly. Indeed, they were all present, and each perfectly formed for her stage in development.

The problem was that it would be really hard to close up the chest and abdomen once they put all of the organs back in place. She didn't have a diaphragm, so they would have to construct one.

He offered for me to come back in March for an ultrasound. He said that he would conference with his peers and the pediatric surgeon and get their opinions on what, if anything, could be done.

This was a far cry from what we had heard in November.

Though that would seem like great news, it was met with great anxiety. Who would know what implications would come with any surgeries should we decide to go that route? We did not want to put our daughter through anything that would prolong any pain or suffering. Our number one priority was to glorify God in all that we do, and we did not want to interfere with what He had planned for her life. So we desperately began seeking guidance from the Lord as to what we should do. We rejoiced as we knew that God was working miracles in the little things.

2 Corinthians 4: 8-9, *We are troubled on every side, yet not distressed; we are perplexed, but not in despair; persecuted, but not forsaken; cast down, but not destroyed.*

I had taken a few days off from blogging, because I was feeling rather destroyed. The roller coaster of emotions we had experienced in the previous days had become almost too much to bear. I came to the realization that we still had some pretty hard days ahead of us, which deeply burdened me. I decided to skim through some of the other blogs I read regularly and came across this verse in 2 Corinthians.

I have read it many times, and the song "Trading My Sorrows" is one of my favorites. How encouraging it is to know that no matter how the world tries to press us, persecute us, or strike us down, we will never be crushed, abandoned, or destroyed. How do we know this? Jesus promises this in His word.

Even in my darkest days, I have the light of His promises to stand upon.

Thank you, God, for your promises. Thank you for keeping me from being crushed, even when I'm being pressed like I've never been pressed before. I'm feeling pretty struck down right now, and my burden seems heavy. Thank you for picking me up, and carrying me through these days ahead.

Chapter Fifteen

NEW HOPE

There is a special bond between sisters. This concept was reinforced for me just a few weeks after that Shands appointment where we first met Dr. Duff. We were in the car listening to Selah, when our girls shared a special moment.

A song came on, played by Selah, about the Lord's Prayer. I love that song; it is amazing. SaraGrace asked me if we could pray for her baby. She wanted me to pray first, and so I did.

Then it was her turn. I heard the most precious words a mother could hear:

"Dear Jesus, thank you for my baby. But please don't make her go to heaven, because I will be so sad. Amen."

This simple little prayer came from the heart of my three-year-old. Hearing these words spoken in such a tiny voice broke my heart anew. Of course, the water works turned on. But it made me realize again how God was working through the lives of our children, even at 3. My cup was running over to see how much SaraGrace loved her baby sister, even before she got to see her.

Monday, February 21, 2011- When Things Don't Go OUR Way

Anyone who has walked on this earth knows that things aren't always going to go our way. And when they don't, it stinks. Like really stinks!!!

As a Christian, we have heard about God's will. The funny thing about His will is that we are all about "God's will be done" until it doesn't look the same as ours. Then, all of a sudden, we're not so sure about His will.

This has been one of the biggest life lessons I have learned while carrying Faith. I've said it before that when we first found out we were pregnant, and experiencing the first set of complications, I prayed that God's will would be done, even though I was secretly praying that our wills would match. Our heart's desire was granted, but it looked much differently than we had planned. Of course, I knew that God had complete control, but I had to TRUST Him to control it. It is situations like ours that make it sometimes hard to pray that God's will be done.

However, I am learning that if you TRUST Him, you can TRUST His will. Just because it doesn't work out the way that we would like, or what we want, or if it looks differently than we had planned, His plans are PERFECT! He knows how things work out, long before we are even aware of the situation.

When we trust God and His plans, we have to be willing to accept His plans! Even if it's not how we wanted things to turn out. That's the beauty of trusting the Lord with all of your heart. I'm so thankful to know that God's got it all together. Even when I don't! I'm thankful that the Savior loves me enough to care so much about me that He is willing to go before me and hold my hand while I walk through the valley.

⁵ Trust in the Lord with all thine heart; and lean not unto thine own understanding.

⁶ In all thy ways acknowledge Him, and He shall direct thy paths.

(Proverbs 3:5-6)

I wrote this post shortly following that episode with SaraGrace's prayer. This was the hardest trial in my life, but I was learning so much. But there was so much more yet to learn.

It's hard to find things to be thankful for when you feel like you are constantly being held down by the world. But even in the midst of the storms of life, we have so many things to praise God for.

Our next appointment at Shands was in one week, and I was feeling overwhelmed. This truth came to mind and continued to repeat itself in my heart, and I couldn't let it go.

I just felt like I needed to be reminded of those things, so I listed them:

> *My salvation.* *I'm so thankful that God loved us so much that He sent His son to die for our sins. Because of this, I have eternal life and eternal hope through Him. I will never be alone because He will carry me through the days.*

> *My husband.* *I'm so thankful for Rob, and the way he loves me. He is my best friend and I couldn't imagine my life without him.*

My children. They are the light of my life. There is never a dull moment in our house. Though that can sometimes be tough, I would never trade it for anything in this world.

This pregnancy. I have never been one that has enjoyed being pregnant. But I will have to say that even though this has been a tough one, I have enjoyed it the most! I think it's because I have learned not to take the little details for granted, because the fact I can even carry a child is a blessing. Faith has taught us so much, and God is changing lives through her story. I'm so thankful that He has chosen us to be her parents.

My family. We are so blessed to have them close by, and for all of their help with the kids. My kids love their grandparents, and I am so thankful for the life they have given me. My sisters are also a blessing to me. I'm so glad we all live so close and can spend time together.

My friends. A girl can't make it through this life without friends. I have been extremely blessed to have some wonderful friends. Especially my Amy!!! But there are many others as well that have really reached out to us. We will never forget the encouraging words, the hugs, the calls, the emails that have really helped us through the tough days.

Our insurance. We have had a lot of doctor appointments, and it hasn't cost us one cent extra. What a blessing that has been. God has really taken care of us in this area.

I followed it up with this prayer:

Dear Jesus,

Thank you for all of the many things you have blessed me with in my life. I know I deserve none of these things, but I'm so thankful for each of them. Thank you for your faithfulness to sustain us in such tough days. You never cease to amaze me in how you show up on a daily basis. I shouldn't be surprised, because you tell us you are here with us. But I'm thankful for the ways you let us know you're here.

You know my heart's desire is for our daughter to arrive perfectly healthy, and to live a perfectly normal life. What a testimony that would be. However, I know that your will may be different than mine, and if it is, I trust you completely. Even if you choose to take her to be with you, what a testimony that will be! Lord, I will choose to praise you no matter the outcome, because regardless of how the next chapter unfolds, you are still the same AWESOME God! We still have so much to be thankful for. Thank you for loving me!

Amen!

After all this, I prepared once again to go back to Shands. It was amazing how much of a difference a single doctor could make. Three months ago, I couldn't have considered it, after that first painful experience. Now, Dr. Duff gave us hope. We had something to fight for.

Was it easy? If anything, it was worse. It turned our quiet acceptance into an emotional roller coaster of hope versus despair.

Before, we were almost certain we were going to lose her, and we had given it over to God. We'd accepted it.

Now we had hope. And hope can be the most devastating thing in the world. But it was still hope.

Chapter Sixteen

A FIGHTING CHANCE

She had a fighting chance. It was small, maybe too small- but it was there. It was a slim hope, but one that gave us a little bit of light in the middle of all the bad news.

My wife cried as we left that first appointment, but I had a completely different attitude. This was the first time since we first got the diagnosis that we had a little bit of hope, however small. I wasn't going to let that go.

I was going to do what I could to fight for my daughter.

From then on, I went to every appointment. I was an encourager to SaraBeth. We had long talks at night, talking things over, trying to make sense of it all. When one of us would get bitter, the other would be ready to lift them up. We'd point each other to Jesus. I couldn't talk to anyone else but her, so those late nights meant a lot to me.

I knew this was going to be hard on SaraBeth, so I tried to be there for her as much as possible. For me, I shut down. I couldn't be strong for both of us, so I didn't let it get that far. There was a wall around my heart, and I couldn't let it down. I had to pull my family through this, and the only way to do that was to stay strong.

I liked the new doctor at Shands, Dr. Duff. At the appointments, it wasn't always just about SaraBeth or the baby. He made sure to include me, and I appreciated that. I felt like I was more of a part of what was going on.

When we first met him, I didn't really pay attention to his demeanor or his actions. But I do remember him wanting to fight for my daughter. He was willing to do what wasn't easy. A lot of times in that profession, it's all about taking the easy way out- just to terminate.

He was completely different from any other doctor we'd had so far. He was going to do whatever we wanted to do, even if it meant keeping the baby. We knew he was there with us. For the first time, it felt like there was someone else there in the fight for my daughter's life.

The next appointment wasn't until March. When it came, we met again with Dr. Duff, just to see how Faith was doing.

At the time, I worked at the University of Florida as an electrician for Physical Plant, the maintenance department of the University of Florida. It just so happens that Shands is actually on campus, so it was easy to arrange for me to meet my wife for her appointment. I only had to take a few hours off from work instead of a whole day.

I went into that appointment geared for battle. I was prepared to do whatever it takes. Whatever we could do to help Faith, we were going to do it. If there was even a small chance, we were going to save our kid. If you are going to help your kid live, who in their right mind wouldn't do whatever it takes? So yeah, we were going to fight.

We went back for the ultrasound, and once again I got to see my little girl up on the screen. SaraBeth was on the table, and I stood next her, holding her hand and stroking her hair. I needed to be there for her, to give her whatever she needed.

At the same time, my eyes were going from the screen to the doctor. I watched the black and white screen, trying to understand the moving shapes and medical notations. Dr. Duff was right there the entire time, explaining what we were looking at. I listened closely, gathering intelligence for what was sure to be a tough battle to come.

There were definitely signs of improvement. The spine had improved, from being affected down to the pelvis to now being affected only as far as just below the chest cavity.

The doctor also pointed out her organs, showing us how they had settled back into the body.

From all this, it appeared that her condition did not look to be as extreme as they thought. Dr. Duff said that he was afraid the end result would still be the same, though, because it did not look like she had a sternum or a diaphragm. There was no pressure system to make her lungs work.

He still left us with hope, because he was going to talk to a surgeon and see if there was anything to be done. He didn't give us any options, because he wanted to talk with the surgeon first.

I left that appointment, turning the information over in my head. I looked at it from every angle, determining what would be my battle strategy. In this fight for my daughter, where would I begin? Surgery? Wait and hope for the best? Or something else entirely?

Unfortunately, there was little for me to do but wait until the next appointment. I would get more intel, and then I could make my decision.

Dr. Kaden, the surgeon, had an idea of what the diagnosis might be, but he wanted an MRI to confirm it. So a little over a week after that first appointment, we went in for the MRI.

SaraBeth went in for the appointment, and I stayed in the waiting room with her friend, Amy. SaraBeth's sister happened to work at Shands, so she was able to go back with her.

There was nothing to do but wait, so that's what I did. After the MRI, I gave SaraBeth a hard time about fainting in the tube. It made for a good joke in the middle of a tough time.

The report didn't come in until the following week. Even then, I didn't hold my breath for it. Dr. Duff called us to let us know his findings, and he was encouraged at what he found. My wife was glad to hear his report, but I was still waiting. It seemed that Dr. Kaden would be the final authority in this matter, and I wanted his word on it.

This entire ride was an emotional roller coaster. We would get the bad news, and then there would be good news to give us a little hope. I couldn't get on that ride. I still had to be strong for my family, so I couldn't do the ups and downs. I just waited, waiting to hear what the surgeon had to say. Once we got his input, only then could we form a strategy on how we would save my daughter.

All I knew is that I didn't want her suffering any longer than she had to. If we were going to do anything that was going to give her pain, I didn't want any part of it. I wanted God's story, but I also wanted the best for Faith.

Chapter Seventeen

PRELIMINARY REPORT

It was only a few days after the MRI that we got the preliminary report from Dr. Duff, but it felt like an eternity. Those days were an agonizing lesson in patience. I spent them desperately hoping they could fix her. At the same time, I danced between praying for a miracle and wanting God to heal her, and trusting Him even if He didn't.

On Monday morning, I received a call from Dr. Duff about the MRI. His tone was very encouraging, but even so, I held my breath throughout the entire conversation.

I posted the details of the initial report on my blog. I was going to wait for the final report, but I wanted to share what we had found out.

> *Faith's head and brain look perfect! They are normal and healthy. Praise the Lord!*
>
> *Her spine is still curved. They thought she might have spina bifida, but her spinal cord is healthy and intact. Therefore, she is not paralyzed, and they can treat her scoliosis at a later date. Praise the Lord!*

She has a diaphragmatic hernia, which they believe is caused by the Pentalogy of Cantrall. She does have a partial diaphragm, and it is only missing on the left side. Praise the Lord!

Her right lung is perfectly healthy and normal, and her left lung is compressed. This is caused by the abdominal organs that have pushed up through the chest cavity. Dr. Duff says that if they can get those organs resituated, that lung should heal and function as it should. Praise God!

Her heart is 100% inside the chest cavity, and is PERFECTLY HEALTHY. No heart defects were detected. Thank you, Jesus!

Her right kidney is healthy, but they could not see her left one. Dr. Duff explained that there are tons of people walking this earth with only one healthy kidney. He did not feel like this was a huge obstacle. Amen!

Some of her abdominal contents are still outside the body. Dr. Duff wasn't too terribly concerned with that as well. Praise God!

Some of the findings sounded pretty scary on the phone. But the doctor felt like the biggest hurdle at that point was that there was no bony structure, such as a sternum, over the chest cavity. Fortunately, if anybody could fix that, Dr. Kaden could. He was the guru in chest wall and abdominal wall reconstruction.

Dr. Kaden hadn't yet reviewed the report, so we didn't have a full prognosis. Even so, it was still encouraging. I asked Dr. Duff how he felt about the report, and he said he was a little more optimistic.

It was amazing to me to hear this report. The news fell on me like a ray of sunshine. I just couldn't believe it! I couldn't help but praise God, thankful that God is still in the miracle business. We were seeing miracles being performed in our little girl, and what a blessing that is! God is faithful! Regardless of what Dr. Kaden would report, we determined to continue to pray for God's will to be done in the life of our Faith. He was still knitting her together, piece by piece, and what a testament she was to the power of our Father and the power of prayer.

Some said this news gave us a false hope, others said it would draw out the grieving process. I knew that our hope was in the Lord Jesus Christ. Not a doctor, not a cure, not a fix. He would ultimately determine the outcome of Faith's life, and we were grateful to Him that He is faithful. He knew what was best for her, even better than we did. If He saw fit to take her to heaven, we still knew He had been working through her and in her the entire time. We saw with our own two eyes, the miracles that had taken place in her little body, and no one could argue that it was only God, not even the doctors.

It was our prayer that we would have clear direction in decisions that would be coming our way. God had been faithful to provide us guidance and peace thus far, and I knew He would not stop doing that now. We wanted His will for her life and for ours, and we were willing to be a part of whatever He decided.

Chapter Eighteen

MEET DR. KADEN

I can't say that I looked forward to the next appointment, exactly. But I was certainly anxious to get to it. We pulled into Shands, and my heart was beating furiously. I had left the kids with my mom. She was an amazing trooper throughout this entire time, and I don't know what I would have done without her. For every appointment, every need, she was always there, ready to take Cade and SaraGrace, as well as provide anything else we needed.

I wasn't quite optimistic when I walked into that meeting with Dr. Kaden. But I had hope. I was mentally preparing myself for what to expect for Faith. We went into this meeting believing that we would be making plans for surgery, for her care in the NICU. I had my legal pad ready, scribbled with notes on questions I wanted to ask. We were going to go over the long list of questions I had prepared for him, so that I could be prepared for what this life had to give to our daughter.

Of course, Rob went with me. My sister, Kiss, was also there, to help interpret the medical terminology for us. Since she worked in the medical field, she would have a better grasp of what was going on than we would.

Within the first 60 seconds of our meeting, our hopes of bringing home a baby girl were shattered again. None of OUR plans were even heard. Dr. Kaden was there to tell us that he had reviewed our MRI, and he believed that the abdominal repair would be much too great for Faith to survive it.

"My life is saving babies that cannot be saved," he said. But nothing in him believed our Faith was "fixable." This abdominal surgery had been done before, but only ended up with months of multiple surgeries, infections, and had the same outcome- the babies did not survive. He did admit that MRIs are not always 100% accurate, and that doctors were only human, so there was a chance that their interpretations could be off.

The overall opinion was to not really have any plans until Faith arrived. Everyone on our team agreed that ultrasounds and MRIs can't see everything they need to see. And I knew they were battling with the fact that a lot had happened in the last couple of months that was medically unexplainable, thanks to the Great Physician.

After we finished listening to all he had to say, we discussed what would take place after delivery. The plan was to attempt to stabilize her with a breathing tube, so that he and his team could get a full analysis of Faith and all that was going on with her little body. Once he had time to make a full examination and determination, he would go from there. Still, he felt that nothing could be done. It was likely we would end up making the decision to let her go into the arms of Jesus peacefully. We did ask about donating her organs, and he assured us that someone would be contacting us with that information.

We were able to get a confirmed C-section date. Although we had set a date already, it had to be adjusted for a day when both doctors would be available. Faith would be born Thursday, May 19th at 9:30 am. That was less than 6 weeks away!

We also definitively decided that Faith would be delivered at Shands, based on the doctor's recommendation. I was completely turned over to Dr. Duff for care. At Shands, she would have access to immediate care when she was born- if she survived.

I felt as if the calendar had turned back to November 15th, 2010, when we first received the news that our child did not stand a chance. So much up and down, hope and no hope, and we sat there once again with the wind knocked out of us and all we had once hoped for.

Needless to say, it was not a good night. I know we had so many things to be grateful for, and believe me, we didn't take any of those for granted. But, the last thing we wanted to accept was that we would not know anything until she got here.

While we did not understand why it seemed as though we had come so far, only to be back at square one, we did understand that Jesus said, "I am the resurrection, and the life; he that believeth in me, though he were dead, yet shall he live: And whosoever liveth and believeth in me shall never die." (John 11:25-26a) We believed this with all our hearts. Our God is sovereign. He is perfect. We wanted Him to be glorified through any and all decisions that were made for our daughter.

We did not lose hope, because our hope comes from God and God alone. We believed that He could perform miracles, as we had already seen time and time again. But we also trusted Him. We were trusting that He alone knew what was best for our daughter, trusting Him and giving Him the glory for all that He had done in and through Faith.

We would choose to rejoice if He did, indeed, decide to take her from us. We would rejoice that she would live eternally with the Father who could love her far better than we could. We would rejoice that she would never know the pain and the suffering this world would have offered her. We would rejoice and say "How Great is our God!"

I knew that God was still in control, and He knew the plans He had for all of us, including Faith, and He promised us that they are plans to give us hope and a future. We knew that our hope could not come from a doctor, an MRI, or a surgical plan, but it must come from God. God's plans might be for Faith to simply be born into His arms, and if that was the case, we would be given hope and a future in the Kingdom of Heaven.

We were not going to lose our trust in Jesus. Just because things didn't go our way, it didn't mean God let us down. It was not the end, only a stepping stone to grow Faith, and grow our faith in Him. Sure, I felt like I had been beaten down, but I knew He would pick me up, carry me through this fire, and see me through to the other side.

I asked for specific prayers that day, as we were tired, emotionally spent, and were feeling weak. I felt like I was being overcome by the burden of our situation, and I was failing as a mom, a wife and just everything else I was supposed to be. Satan was on me like white on rice, and I was trusting in Jesus to take him out!

Rob and SaraBeth on their wedding day- July 12, 2002.

Sarajo and Dexter O'Steen (SaraBeth's parents)
with Rob and SaraBeth at their wedding.

Rob with his dad, Andy Mackney on a
Christmas hunting trip in 2012.

SaraBeth with her best friend, Amy.

The necklace Rob gave SaraBeth
for Mother's Day 2011.

SaraBeth with her mom and sisters and niece. L to R:
Brinley, Beas, Kiss, SaraGrace, SaraBeth and Sarajo.

The hostesses for a Day to Honor Baby Faith:
Back row- Sarah Beck, Julie Bryan, Amy, Robyn Stanley.
Front row- Kiss (Christen), SaraBeth and Beas (Melinda)

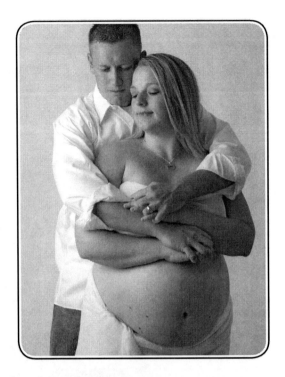

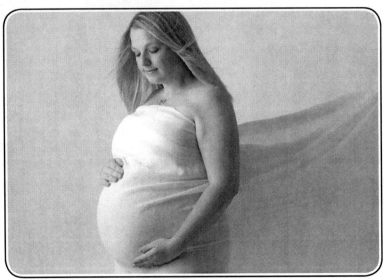

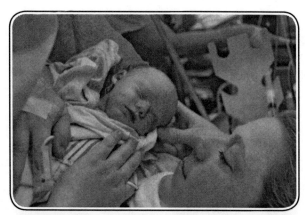

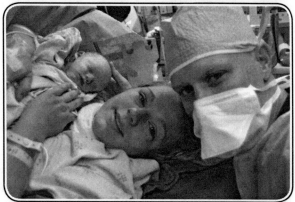

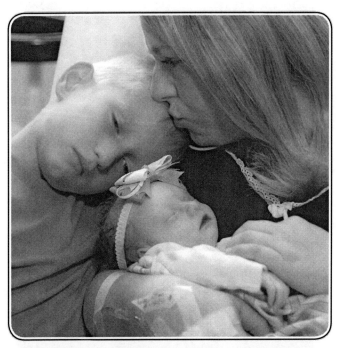

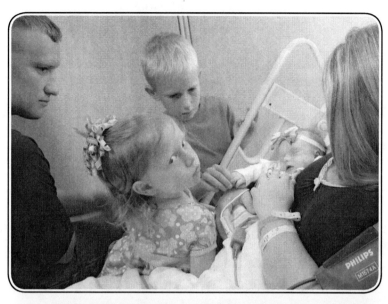

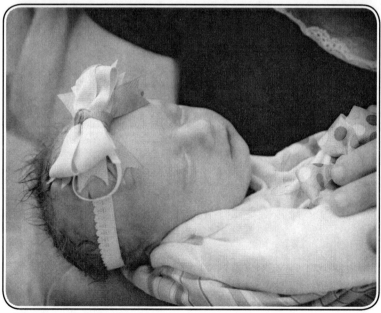

The Vaughn Family- Easter 2013

The Volpes and Vaughns annual gathering
at Disney World- June 2013.

Rob and SaraBeth organized a 5K team in Faith's
honor for a local crisis pregnancy center- November
2013. The team name was Faith, Hope & Run.

Chapter Nineteen

I HAVE DECIDED

Monday, April 11, 2011 – I Have Decided

Yesterday was more emotional than usual. I'm not sure what was different, but I really struggled. We made it to church, just in time for my favorite part- the singing. I love to sing praise and worship songs, and I just look forward to that every week.

We sang "I Have Decided to Follow Jesus." I have heard this song a million times, and can sing it from memory. But it never hit me like it did yesterday.

I have decided to follow Jesus.
I have decided to follow Jesus.
I have decided to follow Jesus.
No turning back, no turning back.

It's easy to decide to follow Jesus, but where it gets hard is the "no turning back." I sat there yesterday, unable to sing through the tears because I thought back to November 15th, when Jesus revealed to us what He was calling us to do. That was the easy part. But truthfully, there are days when it is so unbearably hard, that I want to tell Him I want to turn around. It is too hard. I just can't do it. As I sat thinking about that yesterday, His gentle spirit reminded me of something.

What if Jesus turned back? He knew what He was about to face. He even asked his Father to take the cup if he could. But He remained obedient, and aren't we all so glad He did?

I have committed to following Jesus, and WILL NOT turn back. He has graciously carried us through these days and nights, and He won't let go now. It is hard. It's going to get harder. But He promised us this:

> *⁶ Being confident of this very thing, that He which hath begun a good work in you will perform it until the day of Jesus Christ: (Philippians 1:6)*

He's started something in the life of Faith, and He will be faithful to complete it.

Chapter Twenty

A CHILD'S WISDOM

The wisdom of a child is like nothing else. It is as though their innocence strips away all the distractions we as adults face, allowing them to perfectly see what's there.

We had one such moment while driving home one night. It had been a hard road, and we were getting worn down. I was still reeling from all the ups and downs. The road we were traveling was filled with so many questions. We had never been on this road before, and we had never before imagined that one day we would. There is no one who can give us answers, except the Good Lord above. But that can also mean a lesson in patience, because His answers aren't always immediate. It would be nice if they were, but sometimes we just have to wait.

It was hard, this waiting and not knowing. The fact that we just *didn't know*, many people seemed to take as an offense. Didn't we *know* that God would heal our baby? After all, we were asking for all this prayer- obviously, God was going to do *something*, right? So just have faith! There was no need to make all these arrangements, either for the surgery or for her funeral, because *of course* God would answer our prayers.

I didn't know how to answer this. God would answer our prayers, sure- but would it be what we prayed for? God could heal her- but *would* He? These questions nagged at my mind. I lost sleep over it, because I wanted to make sure that in our efforts to be obedient to God that we never give anyone reason to doubt the power of our Lord.

Yet, we knew that we were doing the right thing. We were asking all these prayers, certainly, but we also knew that God's ways are not our ways. God's plan may not have been to heal her- and we had to be okay with that. But so many times, we were told that we had little faith, for not believing that God would heal her.

Despite our assurance that we were doing right, we still struggled. The questions didn't help. We prayed for a miracle, trying to believe that God would perform it. But there is a difference between believing God *can* perform a miracle, and knowing that He is *going to do it.*

As a parent, obviously our heart's desire was to bring home a perfectly happy, healthy baby girl, who would aggravate her older siblings in the way SaraGrace has aggravated her brother. I would love to be able to look forward to (or dread) the sleepless nights, bringing her to work with me every day, trying to make up with her what I have lacked with the others.

But one thing we desired above our heart's own wants; above our need to rescue our baby; above the gut feeling that the world needs to see a miracle; above the fact that so many people were praying for our sweet daughter- we desired to trust God with everything we had, that His will is perfect, and that HE will get the glory in all of the details of that May 19th.

That can be very scary. His will may not be the same as ours, and we would not know that until that day, even if then. But we always want to be obedient to what He has called us to do, and that is to *trust* Him. We did not doubt for a second that He could heal our baby girl and make her whole. We *know* that He could have. We had seen Him do so much already, but what we didn't know is what HE desired in the life of Faith.

As I struggled with this, we prayed, and even sought counsel from Bryan. Our pastor friend reminded us of Jesus' prayer in the garden, before He was arrested.

Luke 22: 39-44, *"And he came out, and went, as he was wont, to the Mount of Olives; and his disciples also followed him. And when he was at the place, he said unto them, Pray that ye enter not into temptation. And he was withdrawn from them about a stone's cast, and kneeled down, and prayed, saying, Father, if thou be willing, remove this cup from me: nevertheless, not my will, but thine, be done. And there appeared an angel from heaven, strengthening him. And being in agony he prayed more earnestly: and his sweat was as it were great drops of blood falling down to the ground."*

Jesus even asked his Father to take the cup from Him, if it was His Father's will. But then He said, "Nevertheless, not my will, but thine, be done."

We prayed this prayer time and time again. If it be His will that this cup should pass from us and our family, we pleaded that it be done. But, regardless, His will, not ours. I do not want anyone to doubt, for even a second, that our God is *able*. He is able to give, above and beyond, all that we ask. (Eph. 3:20.)

That Friday night, as we were driving home, Rob and I were discussing these verses, and our conversation with our friend. Then from the backseat, a little voice piped up. It was as if God intervened, giving us confirmation that He was in control, and He used the innocent wisdom of a child to do it.

"Mommy, God is using Faith dying to show people how powerful He is. And even if she doesn't die, everyone will still see how powerful He is. He has picked our family to show His power." 7-year-old Cade amazed us with this little bit of wisdom.

As tough as those days were, it was moments like these that made me cherish my Savior even more. All that He was doing in the lives of our young children was such a blessing. And to see such confidence in Jesus, as Cade showed that Friday, it challenged us even more to be confident that we can trust in His plans, regardless of what that may look like for us.

Chapter Twenty-one

A Dress, a Birthday, and Easter Sunday

Life is all about the little things that matter. A few days before my birthday, my mother took me shopping for a new dress. Easter was coming up, and of course, every girl likes to have a new dress for that special Sunday. This year was especially meaningful for me. It would possibly be the only Easter I would get to experience with Faith, and I was determined to be joyful.

This girl's day was just what I needed. It was sort of cathartic; to be able to go out and pretend that everything was normal. Just myself and a few other girls, out for a shopping trip. Nothing more.

Besides my mother and me, my two sisters and my Nanny also went with us. I had SaraGrace, and Cade stayed with Rob. I imagine they went to have some "guy time."

We got to the mall, and the group split. Nanny doesn't get around very well, so she immediately went to find a seat in the mall. We would do our shopping and meet up with her again later, once she had rested. My two sisters, Beas and Kiss, wanted to do some shopping, so they went off on their own, with plans to meet up after we were all done with our shopping.

My mother and I went ahead to the maternity store, SaraGrace in tow. At the store, SaraGrace settled in, content to play with my phone while Mommy shopped.

I looked around the store, eying for that perfect dress. I wanted something specific. This was to be my Easter dress, but it was going to be so much more. In the event that we lost Faith, I wanted something special to wear for her funeral. I didn't want to have to look for something then- clothes shopping would be the last thing on my mind at that point.

This also meant that not only would the dress have to fit my swollen 8-month-pregnant body, but that it would need to be suitable for after I'd had the baby, as well.

Then there was the color. I knew I wanted something bright, especially to remember Faith by. I didn't want to wear drab colors to my daughter's funeral.

Nothing worked. I tried on so many dresses at that store, determined to find the right one. I was also determined to enjoy this occasion. But as so many fabrics and patterns passed through my fingers, despair set in, washing my joy away.

I *needed* that dress.

It was such a silly little thing, to want it so badly, but it was a huge moment for me.

That poor salesperson. The clerk was doing her best to help me, picking out dresses she thought might fit, but without quite knowing why. A few other ladies were in there trying on dresses, and I couldn't help but notice their joy. No dark clouds rimmed their horizon.

The despair rose, and finally the dam broke. Hormones and a heavy heart formed a well of tears that spilled over onto my cheeks. In between halting breaths, I explained to the clerk what I wanted, and why. The poor lady didn't know what to do, but she did her best to help me. I felt like such an idiot. My circumstances certainly weren't her fault.

In the end, I walked out of that store empty-handed. I was disappointed in God- after all this, couldn't He at least have provided a beautiful dress? We were being asked to go through all this for our daughter; surely it wasn't too much just to ask for a pretty dress to wear.

More than that, though, I was disappointed in myself. I was supposed to be this strong Christian girl, ready to show the story of God's love to the world, and how His plans are perfect. Yet, here I was, bawling over something as silly as a piece of clothing.

My mother is not one to give up easily. She was determined to find me that perfect dress. When I broke down, she remained strong, marching me off to look in another store. My mother will stop at nothing to ensure her children's happiness.

It was at this next store that I found *the* dress. Splashed with peacock colors of teal blue and bright green, it was far from drab. It wasn't maternity, but still fit over my swollen belly. Best of all, it would continue to be a great fit even after Faith was born!

Relief washed over me as we purchased the dress and matching shoes. Finally, in the midst of it all, I could still be beautiful. Again I was reminded at how God cares even about the little things. It was a small thing, shallow to some, perhaps, but to me, it meant the world.

We met back up with the others, who exclaimed over the dress I had gotten. I couldn't wait to get home and show it to my husband, and even more, to wear it for Easter Sunday.

I'll never forget that Easter Sunday, or the week prior. It started with my birthday, which my amazing husband went out of his way to make sure was special. We celebrated with dinner at my parents'

house, where she served all my favorites. We loaded up on chicken and dumplings, acre peas, squash and onions, and brown and serve rolls. We concluded the meal with a cake specially made by my fabulous Aunt Wimmy. It was topped with a cream cheese icing, and it was the best!

Afterward, we had the gift-giving. There was the usual assortment of gifts. Maternity clothes from my parents as well as my sister and her husband. Pajamas from my Nanny, and spending money from Granny. My other sister, Kiss, gave me a handmade quilted tree skirt, which she'd had monogrammed with all of our names, including Faith's. I knew I would treasure this one for years to come.

But the one that meant the most to me, the one that I still treasure to this day, was Rob's gift. It came last in the pile of gifts, and Rob handed it to me, grinning with this self-satisfied expression. He was quite proud of himself.

The necklace was simple enough. A circular pendant hung from the chain, in which a tiny cross hung freely. But what made it special were, alongside the cross, the three tiny birthstones. On the pendent itself were inscribed three names.

Cade. SaraGrace. And- Faith.

One for each of my children, including the one we were fighting for at this very moment.

Rob even thought ahead, using two birth stones for Faith. We had one for May, but in the event that she came early, he also included one for April. We could easily switch them out for whichever ended up being the correct one.

This special gift brought tears to my eyes. Throughout this entire pregnancy, I'd felt so little of the joy that most expectant mothers feel. There was so much hurt, so much worry, it threatened to steal any joy I might have in looking forward to meeting my daughter. Instead of preparing a nursery, I was preparing a funeral. I prayed for a miracle, but expected only heartache. I was going to lose my daughter.

That mother's necklace reminded me that even if the Lord called Faith home, she would always be my daughter. I would always remember the little girl I'd carried, but never got to know.

I didn't think anything could ever top that, but little children definitely have a way of shooting straight to the heart.

Thursday was my actual birthday, just a few days later. Rob woke Cade up early and together they created a card for Mommy. Colored in marker, a rainbow and a heart graced the front, while a banner proudly declared, "Happy Birthday, Mommy!" in childish lettering.

Written in red marker, the childish handwriting continued inside, and it was this that touched me the most. Cade wrote, "I love you and pray for you every day!" Hallmark couldn't make a card that sweet! It touched my heart to know that my own little boy was praying for me.

Easter Sunday was right around the corner. It's not my absolute favorite holiday, but I do enjoy it, and I love the meaning. We had our own family celebration in the morning with the "Easter Bunny" goodies, quickly followed by church. Lunch was at my parents' house.

Before lunch, we upheld a longstanding tradition for family pictures. We get them once a year, my sisters and I taking turns playing photographer for each other's families. My husband dresses up just one day a year, and Easter it is. We managed to corral everyone and get a few good snapshots in before the boys, grownups included, dashed away to shed their dress clothes.

I have always loved the holiday, but that year, it was something new to me. Both Easter and Christmas both came to mean something different. We as Christians take for granted the magnitude of the gift of salvation. I came to realize that even though I was heartbroken, sad, and sometimes mad, God knew exactly how I was feeling. The difference was, He *chose* to give up His Son, and I couldn't think of one person worthy of my child's life. I realized that God does care about each of us, and that though we often think He can't relate, He can. He hurt so much to see His Son bear the sins of the world, He turned His face away. He knew what it was like to give up a child.

Put in that perspective, maybe it wasn't so much to ask to give up my own child, after all.

All for God's glory. He was writing my story, and the end was yet to come.

Baby showers are every pregnant woman's best friend. Most likely, she hasn't yet been able to stock up on things that every baby needs. Diapers. Baby wipes. The usual assortment of bath supplies, maybe even tucked inside an infant bath.

What do you do when you don't expect your child to live even for a day?

A baby shower just didn't seem right. As Faith's mom, I wanted her life to be honored and celebrated, just like any other baby. It wasn't about the gifts. After all, we knew that if she were to survive, we were looking at a long road in the NICU.

A dear friend, Sarah, came up to me at baseball orientation. She told me that she and a group of my dearest friends would like to host a day to honor Baby Faith. My heart melted. She told me that they had already talked about it, but wanted to make sure I was okay with it. We set a date, picked out some colors, and they ran with it.

The invitation was one of the sweetest things I have ever read. To see Faith's name, and to know that my friends wanted to honor her life, just warmed my soul. They wrote the sweetest letter on the back, telling of our story, and saying the most encouraging things about my family and the road we were on. Instead of the usual baby shower items, a note for guests suggested alternatives, such as things for us to do as a family- gift cards to restaurants, bowling, movies, spas, etc. What a spirit of thoughtfulness that went into her day.

As I prepared the guest list, I added the names of our closest friends and family. We showed up that day, praying I could hold it together.

There was a spread of food like no other! As it was time for the gifts, the love I felt that day grew. God reminded me just how loved our family was, how loved Faith was. We got gift cards to movies, to Chuck E. Cheese, books, spa baskets, spa gift cards, journals, and even some cash to go towards taking our family to Disney. It was all things that would be comforting to our family, regardless of the outcome of Faith's birth.

Picture-taking followed. In a moment that was sentimental for me, I got a picture with each of the guests. The day before Faith was born, many of these wonderful ladies changed their online profile image to that picture to honor our family.

The outpouring of love of our friends was overwhelming, probably one of the most memorable days of my life. I know it wasn't easy for them, and truthfully it was probably awkward at times. But true friends step outside of their comfort zone to help out and love one another, and that is exactly what happened that day.

This outpouring of love helped to bolster my flagging spirit, giving me strength for the days and weeks ahead.

Chapter Twenty-two
MOTHER'S DAY

Most expectant mothers plan a maternity shoot in anticipation of the arrival of their little one. They take pictures of the mother, accentuating the bulging belly. Then after the baby is born, typically one of the first actions is a newborn shoot to get pictures of the adorable little one. Everyone wants a picture.

I knew I would not get those pictures. Even if Faith survived, there would be no adorable naked little baby sitting on a cloud of fleece. I would not be able to capture those first moments of bliss.

A maternity shoot is done in anticipation of those newborn pictures. I didn't have much to look forward to, so why should I get these pictures? It would only be a reminder of more heartache.

Besides that, I am a self-conscious person. There was no way I could bare my belly to a photographer, much less to everyone else who would be dying to see these pictures. Maternity shoots focus on the belly, and mine was over huge, I felt. Doesn't every pregnant woman feel that way?

I'd heard of Now I Lay Me Down To Sleep, but never before considered it. I saw it first spoken of in the blogs that I read, about the babies and mothers who had had complications.

Now I Lay Me Down To Sleep is a non-profit photography organization. Their purpose is to provide the gift of remembrance to those who have lost their baby. Their classic black and white photos speak not of loss, but of the joy of that baby, however long it lived. Since the organization's beginnings in 2005, they have provided thousands of families with the memory of just a moment of happiness, however brief. It's a memory of that child's life, not a morbid celebration of their death. Many of the children pictured have already died, either stillborn or having passed away moments after birth. These pictures serve as a reminder of the joy that child brought, even amidst the sorrow.

I didn't realize all this at first. When I read about them months before, I thought it was morbid to be taking pictures of babies who had died.

Then I was faced with the prospect of losing my own child. All of a sudden, I knew I wanted something to remember Faith by. I couldn't think of a better way than this.

When we got closer to delivery, Amy looked them up and found that the local director is from High Springs, where my own kids go to school.

The name of the studio sounded really familiar, but I couldn't quite put it together. I called Chontelle Brown on the number listed on the website for the organization. Come to find out, she owns Cotton Blossoms Studio. Her daughter is in Cade's class, and when they were in Kindergarten they went to the pumpkin patch. She took pictures of all of the kids and gave the parents one. That is where I recognized the name. As I began to talk to her, she was already aware of our situation because of Cade talking about it in class.

Incidentally, she works at Shands, the same hospital where I was being seen. In fact, she works indirectly with Dr. Kaden, so she already knew him. Again, God cares about the little things.

She offered to do the maternity shoot for us, and so almost two weeks before Faith was born, we showed up at her studio next to her house. After some considerations, we had decided to include the whole family. We coordinated outfits in a simple white and denim.

From the moment we arrived, Chontelle made us feel at home. She was great with the kids and helped to make me feel relaxed. After a bit, she asked me to change, preparing to do bare belly pictures. Inside, I was dying. Although I felt like a million bucks, I just knew I didn't look it.

Again, Chontelle came through, making it so much fun for me. At one point, Rob stood behind her as she took a picture of me in some type of cloth, belly bared for all to see. From Rob's vantage point, he was able to see the picture as it came up on the camera screen, and he couldn't believe how beautiful it turned out.

Then she took one of just Rob and I, which turned out to be a favorite of mine. The look on our faces is of love for each other and our daughter, yet you can see a touch of heartbreak as well.

Once we were done, we walked over and sat on her front porch with her and her husband. We stayed for quite some time just visiting.

I couldn't wait to see the proofs, and within a couple of days they were finished and she sent them to me.

I was in love. As I looked through the pictures, I was amazed at the transformation. Despite the diagnosis and all the complications, I had been blessed with perfect health throughout the pregnancy. I always felt wonderful, and carried this peaceful expression on my face. There was heartache, but I knew God was in control, and it showed.

I am a self-conscious person. I almost always hate a picture of myself. But I could find nothing critical at these maternity pictures. They were so beautiful, bare belly and all. As a matter of fact, the picture of me and my bare belly was used on the card we handed out at the hospital, and the front of Faith's memorial book at her service.

Friday, May 6, 2011 – Mother's Day

Mother's Day has always been a special day to honor our mothers and grandmothers. We have always made a big deal of it in our family. The big Sunday lunch, the cards, the gifts, but most importantly, the time we would spend together.

I couldn't wait to become a mother and get to stand up in church when they ask all of the mothers to stand. I remember my very first one. I was about 8 weeks from having Cade, and couldn't imagine how precious being a mother was really going to be.

I would have to say that the gift of motherhood is one of the greatest gifts the Lord has blessed me with. I never imagined I could love someone as deeply as I love my children. I remember when I was pregnant with SaraGrace, I was so worried that my heart just couldn't love anyone like it loved Cade. But you know, my heart made room for her, just like it did Cade.

As I think about Mother's Day this year, it means so much more. It's not about celebrating me, but about celebrating the gifts that God has given me in my children. This may be the only Mother's Day that I am a mother to 3 children here on earth, but it's the most precious, as I look at how my perception of motherhood has changed over the last year. It was something I took for granted. I cherish the tender moments I spend with each of my children, even the craziest of days, when I feel like I am at my limit. I have learned to stop and take the time to thank the Lord for the gift of getting to experience those days.

We have gotten to witness our children praying diligently for their sister on a daily basis. We have witnessed Cade giving us profound messages that he has learned through our situation the last few months. All of these are lessons that we, as parents, could not have taught them ourselves. As a mother, it is so sweet and tender to see them grasping what God is doing in their lives, and our lives as a family. Nothing will ever replace these memories that we are making together.

So much of our days have been focused on the possibility that we may not get to experience things with Faith that we have our other children. But the Lord has made it ever so clear that we are not guaranteed tomorrow with the children we have here on earth either. When you stop and think about that, it makes you see a bigger picture.

I have been blessed with the most wonderful mother and grandmothers that a girl could ever ask for. I have also been blessed by the most wonderful children. So this Mother's Day, instead of focusing on what might not be, I am going to focus on all that has been given to us, including the most precious 9 months we have had with Faith.

Hug your mothers, your grandmothers, and your children extra tight this Mother's Day, and take the time to say a prayer of thanks to our Heavenly Father for all of His wonderful blessings.

Our last ultrasound was just a week before Faith was born. Rob went with me to the appointment with Dr. Duff. The appointment went much the same as the others. These office visits were becoming too familiar.

Dr. Duff pointed out the vernix floating around, which was an indication of lung development. We watched in wonder as Faith opened and closed her mouth in practice breathing.

The appointment was short, but no less significant. I remember thinking as I looked at that screen that this was possibly the last time I would ever see her kicking around so happy. She was oblivious to all that was wrong with her, and seeing her do all of those things allowed me to temporarily imagine she was perfect. She did all of the things she was supposed to. This gave me a tiny bit of hope, but more than actual fact, it was in part the imagining that she was perfect.

Chapter Twenty-three

THE LAST 48 HOURS

The last 48 hours of my pregnancy. Most women don't know when their darling baby will be born. At times, I think that lack of knowledge is a luxury.

There are days that it seemed like I had been pregnant forever, yet on the other hand, I found it hard to believe that it was almost over. In just two days, we would look into those sweet eyes for the first time. I was willing to bet that they'd be blue, just like her siblings.

I was filled with so many emotions, but through it all, there was peace. This entire pregnancy had been so up and down, filled with worry and heartache. Yet, peace continued to fill my heart at every turn, knowing that God already orchestrated all of the details.

As always, I blogged what was on my heart. Already, it had grown far beyond its original intentions. It had become a lifeline for me as I recorded our trials, heartaches, and even the joys. The encouragement continued to pour in from my readers in the form of cards, emails, comments, and phone calls. I read each comment and email as it came in, and every word was a comfort to my wearied spirit. I responded to each one as much as I could. Even those that I couldn't get to, they didn't go unnoticed, and I couldn't begin to describe how much I appreciated the outpouring of love and support that was given our family. So many people were walking this road with us, uplifting us in prayer.

Two weeks earlier, Cade did something profound, which sticks with me even now. That morning had been rushed and he didn't get his medication, which he has to take for ADHD. Without it, he gets incredibly moody and nearly uncontrollable.

When I arrived at the school later to pick him up, his teacher indicated she wanted to talk to me. I just knew he'd had a rough day. But it was a very different story I heard from her, as she told me how Cade got the undivided attention of his class, sharing with them all about his baby sister. He asked them to pray for her, so they had a prayer time.

I was so thankful to her for sharing that with me. When we got in the car, I asked Cade about it.

"I told my class that Faith will probably die, so we need to pray for her," he said. "But I told them we needed to pray for you, too, because you were having a rough time."

He then added, "Mommy, I pray for her every day." I knew he did exactly that. It continued to amaze me to see how God was working in his little life. I still don't know the impact this experience would have on him, but I know that God was doing a mighty work.

Everywhere I turned, I could see God's hand. There was heartache, but I could still see His provision, even in the little things. I was now completely under the care of Dr. Duff, who turned out to be a blessing from above. I had been so anxious about switching doctors and hospitals, but God is so faithful to provide what you need when you need it. Dr. Duff is so compassionate, kind, and caring. He made the change pleasant.

I have always been the biggest baby when it comes to pain. In response, Dr. Duff was so accommodating. Unlike the previous doctor, he was very supportive of the decisions that we had made as a family. He was also instrumental in communicating with all of the doctors that would be on board Thursday. Even now, I'm still so thankful for all he did for us!

Soul Surfer was another big moment that week. I had been looking forward to seeing it, and the kids were all too excited to see a shark bite somebody's arm off.

God's timing is impeccable. As the movie starts, Bethany is sitting in youth group, where they are talking about perspective, and how when you are so close to a situation, it's hard to see what is really in front of you. Her youth leader, played by Carrie Underwood, shared a verse with them, telling them that when they can't get perspective, or understand a situation, that they can trust God's plans.

The verse she shared was out of Jeremiah: "For I know the plans I have for you, declares the LORD, plans to prosper you and not to harm you, plans to give you hope and a future." (Jeremiah 29:11, NIV)

Rob shot me a glance and said, "Wow!" Was it just coincidence that they brought up the same verse we'd chosen for our daughter's struggles?

As we watched this young teenager overcome such a trial in her life, it reminded me that the Lord always has us in the palm of His hand. We just have to let go, and let Him do His thing.

Sunday morning soon followed. It's something I always look forward to anyway, just because I love going to our church. But through this trial, I came to love it even more. We would go in and sing the praise and worship songs, and I would stand amazed at feeling Faith leap inside my belly. It was a reminder that we have so much to be thankful for, even in the midst of trial.

I thought about the freedom we'd been given by the sacrifice of Jesus on the cross; that if He hadn't suffered through that trial, eternity in heaven would not be a possibility. Romans 8:28 says that "we know that all things work together for good to them that love God, and to the called according to His purpose."

Thursday drew closer, and I felt my weariness grow. Monday was tough. It was my last doctor's appointment. Afterward, as I was driving to pick up the kids from school, I listened to my Selah CD, and the song "Oh, Draw Me, Lord" came on.

My heart broke. I cried out to Jesus, asking Him to draw us closer to Him during the next few days. I begged for Him to give us the strength and the courage for what lay before us. I asked Him to take the nerves from me, so that we will not lose focus on what He is going to do.

Even as I poured out my breaking heart in this prayer, I had immediate peace. He whispered in my ear, "I'm right here. I haven't gone anywhere."

I knew that the next days, even weeks, would not be easy, but I also knew that God would carry us through them. We could not possibly know what would happen on Thursday, but He promised that He did.

That week, I made arrangements for my two friends, Christina and Amy, to update my blog on that Thursday. I wanted those who had followed our journey for so long to know what was going on.

I concluded Tuesday's post with these words:

Please continue to pray for Faith, for our family, our children and the doctors and nurses that will be on board with us. God is going to do a mighty thing on Thursday, and as Cade reminded us, He will show His power. I am excited to see what He has in store. Thank you again for all of your love and prayers.

I was as prepared as I was ever going to be. Whatever was going to happen that day, I had peace knowing that God was in it all, even the heartache.

His will be done.

Chapter Twenty-four
THE NEWS

May 19, 2011 – While We Wait...

10:30 AM

> *SaraBeth will be going back very soon for her C-section. Please continue to pray and trust HIM!!*
>
> *Love,*
> *Christina and Amy*

May 19, 2011 – Everlasting Faith

11:58 AM

> *Baby Faith is now resting in the arms of our Lord and Savior. Please continue lifting SaraBeth, Rob, Cade and SaraGrace, and their families in prayer as they continue on this journey!*
>
> *Love,*
> *Christina and Amy*

May 20, 2011 – Our Faith Renewed
3:49 PM

Faith Mackenzie Vaughn was born Thursday, May 19th at 11:13 AM. She was 5 pounds, 5.4 oz, with brown hair. She looked just like her brother and sister. Her Daddy was the first to hold her, then he shared her with her Mama, where she was loved, cuddled and kissed endlessly. She passed away at 11:55 AM in the arms of her Mama. Though her life here on earth was only 42 minutes long, the impact she has made will last a lifetime. I couldn't be more proud to be Faith's Mommy. Though we are sad, we do know that she is in the arms of Jesus. She has been made whole and perfect, and our Faith has been renewed.

Faith's Memorial Service will be held Tuesday, May 24th at North Central Baptist Church. Visitation will be at 9:00 am, with the service at 10:00 am. Graveside will follow at Newnansville Cemetary in Alachua. Everyone is invited to the O'Steen home for a time of food and fellowship afterwards.

Thank you to everyone for the prayers, the comments and emails. They have been so encouraging. We are so blessed by all of you who have walked this journey with us.

SaraBeth

The Gainesville Sun
(Running from May 22nd-24th)

Faith Mackenzie Vaughn was born May 19, 2011 and passed from her Mother's arms into the arms of Jesus just 42 minutes later. Though her life on earth was short, the impact she made will last a lifetime. Her story has been followed many people at www.SaraBethandrob. blogspot.com. She is survived by her parents, Rob and SaraBeth Vaughn, her big brother Cade and big sister, SaraGrace, her maternal grandparents (Dexter and Sarajo O'Steen), her paternal grandmother (Sandy Mackney), her paternal grandfather (Andy Mackney), many aunts, uncles, great grandparents and friends.

A memorial service for Faith will take place Tuesday, May 24th at North Central Baptist Church. Visitation will be at 9:00 am and the service will take place at 10:00 am. Graveside service will follow at Newnansville Cemetary in Alachua. Donations can be made in Faith's name to the Women's Resource Center of Gainesville or the North Central Baptist Church Mission Fund.

Chapter Twenty-five

ALWAYS REMEMBERED; WANTING TO FORGET

There are some days in your life that you just never want to remember. You never want to relive that day again, but it's always there in your memory. It sits like a chest that's never opened, just gathers dust.

May 19, 2011 is one of those days.

SaraBeth likes to remember. I don't. It's too deep. In the pictures, our daughter looks perfect. Whole. That is not how I remember her.

Faith Mackenzie Vaughn was born at 11:13. We had to be at the hospital at 7am, but we were fifteen minutes late. Bryan and Christina were there to wait by our side, along with Amy. My wife's parents would be bringing Cade and SaraGrace a little later, once we got settled in.

SaraBeth's emotions were high, but I remained steady. I couldn't fall apart right now. I knew how much she needed me.

We finally found where we needed to go, and Dr. Duff was right there, calm as always. We met with him, and then the nurse showed us to our room.

We were sent to a common room with several other women. SaraBeth was given a gown and assigned the last bed against the wall. We were already planning on starting out in that main room, but then later we were going to be moved to our own room. But when SaraBeth asked the nurse about a private room, we were told that all the rooms were full. So not only she was going to have to wait here for the surgery, she would also have to stay in this same room for two hours after the fact.

SaraBeth couldn't believe it. The diagnosis for our baby was looking bad, and even though we still hoped for a miracle, we were also somewhat expecting Plan B. We didn't want to have to share the little bit of time we would have with our daughter with a bunch of strangers.

I didn't like it either, but I couldn't do anything about that. My wife was in a panic mode. She had hardly slept the night before, and she was already stressing over the birth. So I just stayed with her, telling her that everything would be okay. It was all I could do.

I stayed with my wife the whole time, doing my best to support her. I didn't think about Faith or her diagnosis. I couldn't focus on that right now, so I shut it away in my mind.

SaraBeth has always hated needles, enough to pass out. I stayed next to her, stroking her hair and telling her it would be okay. I talked to the nurses for her, telling them about her needle anxiety and how she always had problems with it before. The IV was bad enough, but the worst was always the epidural.

They got her set up in the bed and started her with the IV. The nurse had to try it twice before finally getting it, but still SaraBeth didn't pass out.

They had a hard time finding Faith's heartbeat. Even then, that baby was stubborn. Hard to say who she got it from, since my wife and I are both stubborn, but it was probably me. After 20 minutes, they finally found it and told SaraBeth to hold still.

Her sister worked at Shands, so she was able to help SaraBeth get the best doctors for the epidural. She knew it was bad with her other pregnancies, so Kiss made sure the other doctors knew about it. The team of anesthesiologists were incredible; they did everything to take care of SaraBeth and made sure that she was comfortable, so that when it came time for the spinal, it was not so bad.

Dr. Arnold was especially helpful. His caring attitude helped make the day bearable, especially for my wife. He went out of his way to make sure that she was comfortable and taken care of. He stayed the entire time the doctors worked, claiming a place at SaraBeth's head. He would check up on her all through the surgery and after.

The actual surgery ended up being postponed by an hour. We spent that whole time in the main room, waiting. SaraBeth was getting more and more nervous, while I tried to keep her calm.

Our friends and family were in the waiting room this whole time- nearly 60 people by this point. Since we were waiting, the staff allowed them to come back a few at a time. Our friends came in to pray with us, and our other two kids came back every 20 minutes. So for the next hour, those who shared the room with us got to experience church with all the prayers that were said.

Finally, Dr. Duff came in to check on us. My wife explained the problem with the private room. He said that he would make sure we had a private room if he had to take us to his house to do it.

Dr. Burke was also with him. Several months ago, at the first MRI appointment when we got the findings, we had asked about organ donation in the event that we lost Faith. Dr. Duff had called this doctor to ask about that. Dr. Burke talked to the center that does the organ donations, and they said they didn't think it was a good fit. They didn't think that they would be able to use Faith's organs because of her diagnosis.

Dr. Burke was also one of the ones that would help with Faith's care after she was born. He wanted to make sure he knew what we wanted. When he asked if we had clothes for her, Kiss went back to the waiting room and grabbed the dress we'd brought for her, and he made sure that it was ready.

Now it was time.

We were led to the operating room, where we stayed for what seemed like a long time.

Finally, the surgery was finished. They pulled my daughter from my wife's stomach. It was 11:13 AM.

I followed both doctors to the little crib that was sitting nearby, where they evaluated her. Everything in me wanted to run, but I had to see. I came around the doctors and stood next to them, staring down at the little body on the table.

That picture will stay with me for the rest of my life. It is one that I can't bear to remember, but I can't forget.

The diagnosis was worse than we thought. Her chest was completely open; I could see all of her organs. Some weren't even in their proper places. There was nothing the doctors could do. There was nothing I could do. I was her Daddy, and I could do nothing.

Dr. Burke went to share the news with my wife. I stayed to help wrap my daughter. It was all I could do to keep my hands from shaking. But I had to do it. I had to cover up all that was wrong with her. I couldn't let SaraBeth see her like that.

Once she was wrapped up, I handed the baby to SaraBeth. My wife held little Faith, stroking her hair, kissing her cheeks. Faith's face was perfectly formed, without flaws.

"I love you, little Faith, and I am sooo proud of you. I love you..." My wife repeated those words over and over again. There was nothing else to say.

I stood next to them, stroking SaraBeth's hair, rubbing my hands over Faith's tiny head. My hands looked so huge on her. She weighed in at 5 pounds and 5.4 ounces. She was tiny.

Dr. Euliano, one of the anesthesiologists, asked if we had brought a camera. We hadn't, because we were told it wasn't allowed. She offered hers, and then after a few pictures, offered for Kiss to get Christina's camera for more. The doctor somehow managed to print off the pictures she took, and she passed them to SaraBeth's parents before we had even left the operating room.

This whole time the doctors kept checking Faith's heart rate. It continued to slow down, but she held on for a long time. She was my little trooper!

Finally, they told us that she had passed away. Our little girl was no longer with us. She never opened her eyes, or even took a breath. It was like she was sleeping.

It was 11:55 AM. She had lived for only 42 minutes.

Chapter Twenty-six

A DAY TO REMEMBER

It was so hard to let her go, but I knew what a blessing it was for her to be in the arms of Jesus. We had prayed that God would allow us time with her. He answered that prayer. We had prayed that she would go peacefully, if He was to take her home. He answered that prayer. We had prayed for healing. He answered that prayer. She was now healed in heaven with a perfect little body.

The doctors had asked if we would be okay with them doing a form of an autopsy, which required no incisions. It would be just a thorough evaluation to confirm the diagnosis. We agreed, and Rob stayed right there with her. They confirmed that she indeed had the Pantalogy of Cantrell, a birth defect.

Since my surgery was complete, Dr. Duff made sure we were able to go to a private room, where my children and family and friends would meet their angel they had prayed so diligently for.

Kiss went outside to tell everyone about Faith. She met my parents in the hallway, and knew she couldn't face the crowd of people to tell them all that had happened. My dad went in to the waiting room, where he shared that Faith was gone. Not long after that, our doctor went in and shared with everyone all that had happened in the operating room. My dad said he has never met a more humble doctor than Dr. Duff. He said that Dr. Duff told them all what a privilege it was to be our doctor.

Once the doctors had completed their evaluation, Rob and our nurse cleaned her up, and dressed her in her little gown. He brought her to our room, and she was *beautiful*! She looked so peaceful, yet like such a little girl. Of course we had the hair bow for her, and she looked so cute!

Chontelle was in our room waiting for us to take our pictures. Cade and SaraGrace came in and they were such troopers. They both wanted to hold her, and they just looked at her in awe. They checked out her hair, her little hand, and SaraGrace admired her bow. They argued about who she looked like. Chontelle was able to take quite a few pictures, and I'm so glad we were able to do that.

Once she was done, and our family had some time, our parents came in and got the first glimpse of their newest granddaughter. They all bragged about how much she looked like SaraGrace, but with brown hair. No one could believe that she was really gone. Rob did such an amazing job recounting her birth details to them, so that they could experience just a part of her little life. I'm telling you, he was so amazing! God really gave him the strength to carry our family through the day.

Once everyone had a chance to see her, we called the funeral home. We knew it would take some time, so we just sat and took in every detail about her. Cade was able to hold her a couple of times, and he was so proud to be her big brother. He asked some questions, but he was strong, just like his daddy.

Our Father knew we needed a laugh, so He sent in the grief counselor. There was nothing funny about her or what she was sharing, but as she left, she was trying to figure out who was who. Rob, the kids, the Volpes, Aunt Amy, and my friend "Kicken" (Kristen) were all in the room. As the counselor left, she looked at Amy and said,

"And you must be the Grandma!" Amy was none too happy about that, and was quick to inform her she was NOT the grandma. We laughed together about that all night and into the next day.

The funeral home came to get Faith a little after 6:00. Rob and Cade took Faith to meet the director downstairs. It was hard for both of them to let her go, but they knew they had to. Once they came back, we were taken to our room. At the time, Shands was remodeling the OB-GYN floor, so some of the patients were transferred to the newer wing across the street, accessed via a tunnel that ran under the road.

We transferred to our new room, and it was a suite of a room! It was very quiet, and I couldn't help but feel like I was staying in the Marriott. I was starving, as I hadn't eaten since 10:00 AM that morning. Rob and Bryan went and got us some Texas Roadhouse. I devoured a steak and a double order of cheese fries in no time flat.

We were all so exhausted, but I wanted to make sure that I could recount every detail of that day. We hashed it over and over again, and it was so hard to believe the day had finally come to an end. Though it was an extremely difficult, sad day, it was a good day. We knew that Faith had fulfilled her purpose that God had set for her life. We knew that we had done all we could as her parents to give her a chance at life. We knew that we had finished this leg of the race, and that Jesus was right beside us, making sure every detail was accounted for.

May 19th, 2011 is a day that will be remembered by many as the day Baby Faith came into this world, leaving a footprint on the hearts of everyone who knew her.

Chapter Twenty-seven
THE FUNERAL

I never imagined that one day I would be grieving the loss of my child. It was never something I could have pictured. These last nine months had been a battle, and it was all I could do to be strong for my family.

But now... now the battle was over, and I was beginning to break.

I couldn't allow it just yet. There were still things to be done. We had a funeral to go to. I still needed to be strong.

Then I fell apart. We were at the funeral home, a private visitation. Just the four of us. Myself, my wife, and our two kids. It should have been three.

The third was in the casket.

My daughter.

She looked beautiful. There wasn't a hint of imperfection to be seen. Mr. Milam took good care of her.

The kids drew pictures to put in Faith's casket. Cade was quiet, too quiet. SaraGrace, only three years old, couldn't understand. We told her that Jesus took her to heaven, so why was she in that box?

I wanted to help seal the casket. Maybe it gave me closure, I don't know. But as the lid softly clicked closed, there was the stark reality that we had seen her face for the last time on this earth.

The next morning was the funeral service. It had been almost a week since Faith died. Just five days. I still hadn't really processed it. I knew that if I tried, I would break. I couldn't do that just yet. My family looked to me for everything. I was their rock. Rocks don't break.

The casket was at the front of the church, surrounded by flowers. We had decided on a closed casket service, because neither of us wanted people to remember our baby by what was in that box. We wanted to celebrate her life, not what was left of it in the box.

Instead, we framed a picture of Faith and set it above the casket. Everyone could see just how beautiful she really was. They didn't have to see the picture that I saw every time I closed my eyes.

Cade and SaraGrace both received a stuffed bear, a gift from the church. It was a cute moment, and I was glad they were taken care of.

We held a visitation for Faith before the service started. A huge amount of people showed up. It was almost overwhelming at how many people were there to support us.

Through it all, I stayed with my family, doing what I could to support them in this time. I couldn't "fix" their grief, but maybe I could ease it just a little bit.

The funeral was exhausting. I played so many roles that day. I was the grieving mother. I was the proud mother. I was the comforting mother of my two small children. I was the encourager to our visitors. I was the loving wife helping to sustain my husband. I was the greeter. I was...

The list goes on, endless.

I stood at the back of the church and watched helplessly as my dad walked with my mother up to the casket. It was absolutely heart-wrenching. They were sobbing, unable to catch their breath. My mom just shook her head as the tears flowed. My dad held her, trying to comfort her in his own grief. In this moment, I was so thankful for the opportunity to go see Faith's body the day before. The shock of the reality and the smallness was undeniable.

Amy took such good care of me. I will never forget how my best friend was there for me when I needed it most. She and her husband, Byron, saw to anything we needed. They made sure I kept up on my pain meds, prescribed after my C-section.

Finally, the funeral director, Ashley Milam, came and got us when it was time to start. We proceeded into the church.

We started off with a congregational. "How Great is Our God" is a song that continues to have an impact on my life. It is so amazing to know that God still has a purpose. When turmoil hits, all we can do is look above and say, "How great is our God!"

My heart was broken, but I was at peace. I looked at that tiny casket and declared how great our God was. Seeing my husband lift his hands in worship to our Almighty God was a sight that is forever burned into my memory. Michael played the guitar and we all sang.

Then it was Bryan's turn. He began by offering his own thoughts, taken from Scripture. Hebrews 11 was what came to mind for him- the "faith" chapter. How appropriate for our own little Faith!

He then read a letter to Faith, written by Rob and me. Several months after, when I listened to the service recording, I realized what a responsibility we had given him. He was so strong, and he said the most kind words about our family. As his voice shook, my heart broke even more. While we were so sad, we were blessed to have such wonderful friends who cared so much about our Faith. She was special to them, too.

"I Will Carry You" by Selah remains a favorite of mine. When the dark clouds of grief threaten to overwhelm me, I remember the promise contained in this song.

As Kelly sang it that day, I remember continually telling myself that even though I loved my daughter, no one could love her like Jesus. This was something I had to remember, to hold in my heart.

The message that followed was one of the sweetest messages I have ever heard. Pastor Calvin said that sometimes, the Lord has mercy on the parents and heals the child. Other times, he has mercy on the child instead and takes them to heaven.

There are babysitters in heaven, did you know that? I could just imagine Hannah rocking my baby. It was a sweet picture that gave me comfort. Even if that wasn't how it really happened, it still comforted me to know that the Lord would take better care of my child than I ever could.

"A brief life is not an incomplete life. We're not promised a hundred years of life. There are no mistakes with God, He is perfect. Faith's name means to trust, and today this family, and you and I, we choose to trust a perfect God.

"Faith is in heaven with a perfect God. There are the best babysitters in the world in heaven. Hannah who had baby Samuel is in heaven. Jochebed, Moses' mama, is there. The best babysitters in the world are in heaven. Rob and SaraBeth, it is almost as if God said to us, 'This child is so special, if you don't mind, I think I'll raise her myself.'"

One of the things we wanted from the beginning was to convey the message of salvation through Faith's life. We knew there would be some people at her service that may never have another opportunity to hear about the love of Jesus. This would be the only chance for them to hear the true message of the Cross of Calvary. This message was the one that was woven throughout Faith's story. In the end, it was the purpose for her story.

"Whatever you do, don't just get half the message today." Pastor Calvin's words, and even more the message, washed over me, reaching into my heart as a healing balm. "Faith is alive. She's in heaven. You know why she's alive, why she's in heaven? Because Jesus Christ defeated death at Calvary, and because He came out victorious, so did Faith."

He then went into the old, familiar "plan of salvation." We're all sinners in need of a Savior- a mediator between man and God. That mediator, Jesus Christ, provided a way for access to God. All we have to do is call upon Him. Confess with your mouth, believe on Christ, and you "shall be saved."

"Could it be that God is getting our attention in some way?" Could it be? The preacher shared an illustration about the shepherd with his sheep. The sheep don't like to cross a stream; they are afraid of moving water. So what the shepherd will do is pick up a lamb and carry it across. The mother can't stand to see her baby leave, and so she follows, and finally so does the rest of the flock.

Was Faith that baby lamb? My baby, so tiny, so helpless, yet leading us across to follow after the One who gave Himself for us. We were the sheep, hovering on the edge of the stream, hesitant to follow.

The rest of the message continued on, weaving together both the story of our own little lamb, and the message of the Shepherd's sacrifice.

"I'd like for us to bow our heads and hearts in prayer..." There was a silent shuffle as the congregation moved to do as he had asked. The tears still quietly flowing, I held tightly to my husband's hand and lowered my head.

"I would like to say that if you're here without Jesus Christ, the greatest encouragement to this family would be that you would give your heart and life to Jesus Christ. Jesus died on the cross to pay for your sins and to purchase us a place in heaven, which He offers to us as a free gift." Speaking directly to the people now on a personal level, Pastor Calvin once again covered the plan of salvation. He then led into assurance for those who may have accepted it, and the follow-up for what to do next.

Our music director sang, "Lord, I Run To You." As he sang, I watched my other two kids. Cade was so sad, sitting with this solemn look on his face. SaraGrace, only three years old, couldn't understand what was going on. She would lean over and ask, "Mommy, why are you crying?" Her little heart just couldn't comprehend the huge sorrow we were experiencing, but she knew something was wrong.

Cade was my little soldier. He wanted to read a Scripture, so after Michael's song, it was his turn. His Daddy asked him if he wanted help. Cade simply said, "No, I got it."

He walked up from his seat on the second row and stood at the microphone like he had done it a thousand times. I could not have been more proud of him and the example he was. He was so strong, though he was disappointed that God had not answered his prayers. He was sad, but knew that God's plans were greater than ours.

"Hope is faith holding out its hand in the dark, and it is putting faith to work when doubt might seem to be easier. Life with Christ is an endless hope, but life without Him leads to a hopeless end. This is the verse I've chosen..."

He then read from Jeremiah 17:7. His young voice was so strong, so sure. He just knew that God had a bigger plan for his sister. If only adults could have that same steady confidence!

The service concluded after a final song. Our friend, Brad, sang, "With Hope" and then, without further words, Pastor Calvin closed in prayer. "Lord..."

The tears were flowing in streams now. Grief and agony ripped through my broken heart. Bitterness threatened to rear its ugly head. I knew it would be all too easy to give in to it. But weaving through it all like a soft breath in a stormy night, was the peace of God that passes all understanding.

My heart was broken, but I was at peace.

Chapter Twenty-eight

JESUS LOVES ME, THIS I KNOW

Once the service was over, we met every last person in the foyer of the church, thanking them for coming.

As my Uncle Ron came through the line, he said something to me that will never leave my heart.

"The Bible talks about laying up treasures in heaven, and now you have a treasure there," he said. "You will long for heaven even more, now."

This nugget of wisdom has remained with me to this day. He couldn't be more correct! I look forward to the day when I *know* that I will see my baby girl again.

If the service was hard, the next part was even harder. Rob and Bryan together walked to the front of the church, where each grabbed a side of Faith's casket, and carried her out to the hearse.

This was an amazing picture of a Daddy's love, and a true friendship that stands through the hardest of times. To have a friend who can help carry you, and your daughter, through the darkest moments in life is a blessing that is immeasurable.

At this point, I was hurting. Not just emotionally, but physically as well. It had been less than a week since my surgery, and I had been on my feet all day. It was starting to wear on me.

It had been a long morning, but we still had to go to the cemetery. My dad gently helped me into their SUV. Rob and my mom were busy helping get the kids in the car. It was hot, and we had a good drive ahead of us.

I could not wrap my head around the fact that we were really about to bury my daughter. She had been my life the last nine months. I was her ambassador, fighting for her. Every breath I had in me had been spent encouraging someone in the name of Jesus on her behalf, talking to doctors about saving her life, comforting and answering questions from my children.

Rob and I had spent every ounce of energy we had using her story to glorify God in all that we did. What in the world would we do now that she was gone?

As the processional wound its way through my small hometown of Alachua, there was a construction crew from a local company working on the road. They all took off their hats and watched us pass.

The graveside is probably one of the vaguest moments to me. Everything was so hazy by this point. I remember sitting under the small tent, trying to take in every last moment we would have with her.

They were too few.

Pastor Calvin said some words, and to be honest I don't even remember what they were. We prayed and then we each left a flower on top of her casket.

No matter the occasion, every good Baptist service or get-together involves food. This was no exception. We left the graveside service to go to my parents' house, where everyone was already gathered. Members from my parents' church family, along with ours were there, already handling the hostess jobs. By the time we got there, everyone had already gotten food and was taken care of.

I managed to find a seat in a recliner, and someone brought me a plate of food. I nibbled slowly, knowing I needed to eat. I was still recovering from surgery, and my body needed the nutrition.

I tried to visit with the guests who had gathered for our sake, but it was difficult to work up the energy. I was tired, and I was in so much pain.

My friends would each take turns to come sit by me in the recliner. They all told me how beautiful the service was, how special Faith was. Meanwhile, Rob got to spend some sweet time with his own family. His Dad, Andy, was there, as well as his brothers and a few of his friends.

Amy and Christina held everything together for us and my parents. I know I couldn't have done this without them.

My parents equally held it together, though I can't imagine how. They took care of my older two children, seeing to their needs. They played hostess to Andy and his wife all week, and then Rob's brother, who stayed the night with them for the funeral. To top it off, they hosted the gathering after the funeral. Through it all, they held it together for Rob and me. All this, while trying to grieve the loss of their grandchild. I remember how adamant Dad was that the picture of Faith stay at their house. He didn't want to let it go. We brought it to their house from the church, and it still sits there today.

Finally it was time for the guests to leave, and we were left with our close circle of friends and family. Bryan and Christina. Amy and Byron. My parents and my sisters. We sat and recounted the events of the day. It had been so sweet, and I wouldn't have done anything differently. Her service was perfect for her. I am still so glad that we had taken the time to plan out every detail long before Faith was even born.

It had been a hard day, but it was the beginning of healing for me. The gulf that had spanned in my heart was beginning to close. I would always have a hole, and I could never forget my daughter, but I was comforted.

Jesus loves me, this I know; for the Bible tells me so...

Chapter Twenty-nine

HEAVEN IS REAL

Heaven is real. It really is, I promise you. It's the most wonderful place you could ever wish to be, and you're in the arms of the most wonderful person in the world- Jesus Christ.

But when you're a three-year-old child who just watched your baby sister closed up in a box and buried underground, and your parents tell you that she went to heaven- well, it may not paint the most ideal picture. In fact, you might just downright hate it.

SaraGrace did.

I had no idea how much she was struggling with this whole subject. With my adult perspective, I knew that Faith was never really in that box, that it was just her body left behind. Her soul had departed and gone to be with Jesus.

A three-year-old doesn't comprehend the meaning of a soul. So when we said "Faith," she logically assumed that we were referring to the baby in that box.

For several weeks after the funeral, she would say things like, "I hate Jesus," and "I hate heaven." And the most telling- "Jesus stole my baby sister."

Stealing was wrong. And she missed her baby sister.

Thursday on the way home from school was no exception. Nearly a month had passed since Faith had died. We were still trying to cope, to find a new meaning in our life. We were still looking for our "new normal."

Once again, SaraGrace declared that she hated heaven and didn't want to go there.

I turned around, asking, "Why? Why don't you want to go to heaven?"

With a determined pout, she stated, "I don't want to be dead in heaven."

I tried to reassure her. "You won't be dead in heaven, honey. You are alive in heaven. Baby Faith is alive in heaven."

At this, her eyes lit up. "She opened her eyes in heaven?"

I nodded, remembering how Faith had never opened her eyes here on this earth. "Yes, baby, she opened her eyes. She's alive in heaven. She's probably singing songs and playing with Jesus."

She considered this for a moment. Then, "So she's alive in heaven? I'll be okay if I go to heaven?"

"Of course you'll be okay." My words were meant to reassure her, but she had given me pause for thought. We had told SaraGrace that her baby had gone to heaven, but she was associating "heaven" with having to close your eyes, get in a box, and be buried in the ground. I can honestly say that if I thought that was heaven, I wouldn't want to go, either.

Ever since this conversation, SaraGrace talked constantly about Faith, but the negatives disappeared. She now had a much better understanding of what heaven is, and would speak of how Jesus was taking care of her baby sister.

I'm so thankful for the promise God has given us in heaven. I'm so thankful that He cares so much for us that He has gone and prepared a place for us. If we would just receive His gift of Salvation, it's ours for the taking. I pray that each of you will know that heaven is for real!

We desperately needed family time. Two weeks after Faith, and we were still reeling. I guess we still hadn't quite gotten over the shock of it all. We were all still so numb.

For me, I almost didn't know what to do with myself. From the beginning, my baby's life was threatened, and I had spent the last 9 months fighting for her. It was consuming. Now that she was gone, I was adrift. My purpose had been served, and I had nothing left to fight for.

That's not to say that I was in danger of ending my life. I had too much to live for. I wasn't suicidal, or even depressed. I was merely adrift, without purpose. I didn't know what to do with myself.

My sisters knew just what we needed. They and their husbands pitched in to purchase tickets to Disney World. They also sent us with spending money for each of our two kids. Bryan and Christina went with us.

That day was just what we needed. It allowed us to let loose, reminding us of the family we still had. We had lost one, but we still had each other. The smiles we shared on that day bound us together. The laughter broke something in us, a collective dam that we had all built.

It would bring healing, but when a dam breaks, there is destruction. I just didn't realize how much, or what it would cost.

Chapter Thirty

MOVING ON

She would have been one month old today. It could have been her first day in church. Maybe even her dedication.

She would have looked beautiful. She'd be dressed up in a frilly dress. She'd be wearing a big bow. All dressed up for church, ready for everyone to meet her.

I am finding that my rock is beginning to crack. I can't show it, just yet. I see the look in SaraBeth's eyes, and I know she is hurting.

I can't break just yet.

We went to the cemetery yesterday. Is it morbid? I don't know, maybe. But we both wanted to go, just for Father's Day.

How do you celebrate being a father when you just lost a child? You don't. You only grieve.

She was my little girl, my baby. How was I supposed to just let her go?

The funeral is supposed to fix it. It's supposed to give you closure, make you feel better so you can move on with your life. It's like you have the funeral, and then everyone expects you to just be okay.

It's not okay. I don't see how it could ever be "okay."

She would have been one month old. Maybe had her first smile. I never did know what to do with a baby at this stage, but I missed it just the same. Babies don't do much, other than eat and sleep, but I still missed holding her.

God, I missed her. I missed her so much.

The pain grows, a little more every day. Or maybe I'm just less numb. The numbness of losing our daughter is finally wearing off. I thought I knew pain, but I've never known anything like this. Your stomach is in knots, and everything inside you is being torn apart. You're trying to stand on solid ground, but there's a hole at your feet. A canyon sucks you in, and the only thing that compares is the hole in your heart.

I'm still trying to hold it together, but I'm losing the battle. I'm slipping a little more every day. I think that if I just hold on, I will be okay. But I don't have the strength. I'm worn down, and I don't know where to go.

I talk to SaraBeth, but she is hurting just as much. She cries uncontrollably, and sometimes she's irritable. I don't blame her, but I can't reach her, either.

When two people are in that much pain, it's hard to hold on to each other. In times when we should be holding even tighter, we're letting go.

I'm letting go, and I'm falling away.

"After Faith." Strange how everything now seemed to be defined by those two words. Nearly ten months had revolved around her, as I fought for her and then lost her. It had become my life for those months.

Now, we found ourselves having to redefine our life, finding a new normal. It wasn't easy. Even two months later, I was still adjusting.

I needed a way out, just for a little bit. Go somewhere, recoup for an afternoon, and get back in the game.

In the 14 years that I've known her, Amy has always known exactly what I needed. She is the kind of friend that most people never get to experience. There is hardly anyone more loyal, more dependable, or more loving. Our friendship is the epitome of a "true friendship." In all our years of friendship, there hasn't been one life experience that I haven't shared with her. She is one of God's greatest blessings in my life. When I was thinking over all she had done for me these last ten months, I knew there was no way to repay her.

But still, I wanted to do something special for her and with her. The answer was a spa trip. It just so happened that I had a few gift cards for Cloud 9.

It's amazing what you can find while cleaning, and this was certainly no exception. My house has always looked like a mini-episode of the TV show "Hoarders." Yes, I definitely have pack rat tendencies.

We decided it was time for an overhaul, and spent several days gutting the house. We went through closets, bedrooms, every nook and cranny, throwing out what wasn't needed and organizing what was kept. In the end, my husband took three truck loads to the dump.

In all that mess, we came across several unused gift cards, along with the usual scattered change. A couple of these cards were for a nearby spa resort.

I needed to spend some time and get away from everything, and this seemed to be just the way to do it. So I called up my best friend Amy and invited her to come with me. A girl can't go to a spa alone, can she?

Cloud 9 was food for the body, but even more for the soul. With the gift cards, we were each able to get a massage, and it was long overdue.

I left that afternoon feeling renewed and ready to face anything. After the events of the last few months, this relaxation was just what I needed. I went home refreshed, but unaware of the storm that was even then beginning to form.

Chapter Thirty-one

THE DAM BREAKS

The vacation had been wonderful. 6 days of fun and enjoyment, of forgetting all the "before." We were a family, and we could still have fun like one.

It was a time for getting together as a family and spending time with good friends. It had been quite some time since the Volpes had moved to Virginia, but we still kept in regular contact. Getting to spend this week with them in Virginia was a highlight.

In the end, it was the calm before the storm. I saw this vacation as getting back together, our family coming together after so great a trial. I had no idea just how much my family was falling apart.

I had been so strong for a long time, trying to be there for everyone. I was the ambassador for Faith, fighting for my daughter's life. I was the comforter to my other two children, comforting them in their loss. I was the supporter for my husband, helping him through this time.

Who was I to me?

Now, everyone else was moving on, healing. The kids were handling it fine, they were moving on with their life. Rob was quiet, but Rob is always quiet. So I finally allowed myself to grieve.

I withdrew. I was emotionally unavailable. Rob seemed distant, but I chalked it up to him reacting to my emotional wreck. I didn't know what it was then, but something seemed "off."

He was late getting home that Friday night after we got home, and I couldn't help but question. I like to confront things head-on, so when he arrived home, I pulled him into the bedroom and closed the door. It was time for the tough questions.

He admitted things weren't as great as I would have liked to think they were. Weren't they? All this time, I'd had this image of my family- hurt, but not crushed. We'd weathered the storm, gone through the worst trial a person could experience. Yet, we made it through. We were still the strong family. We had determined to stand strong, showing the world what God can do even in a trial.

We were standing strong. But that was a cardboard picture that we showed to the world. On the other side, we were crumbling apart. To the world, Faith was an amazing picture of love and strength in trial. In reality, it became the wedge that threatened to drive us apart.

Statistics say that a good number of couples who lose a child end up divorced. I was determined not to let that happen.

Sometimes, things don't happen the way we determine them. Sometimes, you can't hold back the flood by pretending it isn't there.

And the dam had just broken.

Rob packed his things. He needed to- to do what? What in the world could be more important than his own family? But we weren't a family. We had become strangers living in the same house. His love for his family eclipsed by his own grief, there was nothing to hold him to us. I wanted to do everything I could to hold on to him, but he was already moving on.

There is nothing like standing at your door, watching a set of tail lights disappear into the night. You stand there, wondering what went wrong, how to make it right. It's in that moment that you see all that you didn't want to see, when the world you thought was so perfect is instead falling apart.

Who could I be mad at? God? How could the God of the Universe be so great, asking us to give up our child, and now allow Satan to destroy our marriage? I couldn't believe after everything we'd been through, our testimony we'd worked so hard to build would just disintegrate into another statistic.

Yet, it was happening, right before my disbelieving eyes. As I watched him leave, so many thoughts flashed through my mind. If only's and what if's chorused their demanding voices, steadily chipping away at what was left of me.

I had lost my daughter. Now, I was losing the only man I'd ever loved. Could our marriage be restored, or was it destined to fall into a disgraceful heap, mindless of the story we'd determined to uphold?

In all this, I had forgotten one very, very, important thing: This was God's story, not my own. I was still taking control, determined to write my own happy ending. I had lost my daughter, and so my aching heart determined that there must be a purpose. I was determined to write that purpose.

Taking the reins is always a dangerous thing. You may end up losing the thing you love most.

Friday night was a sleepless night. Other than hospital stays for her pregnancies, and my work early in the marriage, I had never been apart from SaraBeth. In all our nine years of marriage, I had been by her side. Even in the beginning, when I was still trying to party all the time, I tried to be there. I had all the opportunities. These kinds of parties were always full of girls, ready and willing. There was a day, before I knew what following God meant, when I might have taken them up on it. But I wasn't that kind of man.

Christ had made me into a new man, one who would always be there for SaraBeth.

Later, I was there in leading my family to follow God. It took me a bit to figure it out, but I finally knew what was right. We went to church, we did what we were supposed to. We taught our kids about following Jesus. We told people about the power that God has in our life. I know that He does, because he changed my life. We did everything we were supposed to.

We trusted God the whole time and all we got was hurt. Friends said things that hurt. We prayed for a miracle, but lost a child. And worst of all- I was her father and I couldn't fix this. Knowing this ate me alive more than anything. I've always fixed everything in my life. When hard times came for my family, I was the one who stood strong. In each of my wife's pregnancies, the complications and troubles that came with each, I was there. I stayed strong.

But I just couldn't do it anymore. I was done being there for everyone. I was a rock, but this rock had cracks. The cracks were starting to grow, and now the rock was broken. I had tried to be strong for so long, but I had no strength left.

I never stopped to think what would happen. And so I did something I had thought I would never do again. I found someone else. Who was she? It doesn't matter, really. An old flame or a new friend, what difference does it make?

But she was there.

We connected first over Facebook. These social sites aren't all bad. But I'll tell you right now, they can certainly get you into trouble, and so it did here.

She tried to contact me before, but I ignored it. I didn't need anything. I had my beautiful wife, my wonderful family. We had a perfect life.

But now I was vulnerable. I was broken. The next thing I knew I was hanging out with the wrong crowd, doing stupid stuff all over again. I was deeper than I'd ever gone before. This trial in my life had cut me to the center, digging out everything I'd left behind. I was saved in Christ, but I shifted back to who I was before, the old man. When the new man in Christ falls, the old man is waiting to stand up strong.

I couldn't fall apart. I stayed strong, certainly, but I was blinded to what sort of destructive strength this old me would have on my life and my family.

So I made choices, horrible ones. They were ones that nearly cost me my family. I thank God He gave my wonderful wife the ability to forgive, because I know I tore her heart out that day I walked away.

She begged me to come back, trying every tactic she could think of. But I was too hurt, too blind. Both of us had been so focused on staying strong, we forgot to hold each other up, and so we grew more distant. Now, I felt like I was unimportant in her life. She shut me out, and she didn't need me anymore.

So I left, staying at my mom's for the time being. SaraBeth continued to text me. When she couldn't get me to come home, she begged me to come to Cade's football game the next day. She was desperate to keep up appearances for the sake of the kids, just while we worked things out, but I wasn't so sure. I had become so blinded in my own pain that I failed to see the pain I was causing my own children.

I did show up for the game, in the end. I did the usual, hugging and kissing her like always. But there was nothing to it. It was all pretend. The kids didn't notice anything, not at first. We went out to lunch after the game. Just a small family enjoying a meal, right? It couldn't be farther from the truth.

SaraBeth continued to beg, pleading for me to come home. I just couldn't do it. I couldn't keep up the pretense any longer. I couldn't pretend that things were fine when they weren't. So I said no. I even went so far as to tell Cade about it. The kids thought that Daddy was just visiting Grandma Sandy for a few days, but I was tired of *pretending. So I told Cade that I couldn't ever come back home. Mommy and Daddy didn't love each other anymore.*

SaraBeth was furious with me, but I knew I had to tell Cade. I just couldn't pretend. The old man in me was still holding strong, in full control. The old man is the sinful man, the one that has not been washed by the blood of Christ. Only Christ can change a man, and when you block Christ out of your life, you also block that change.

Chapter Thirty-two
"I FORGIVE YOU"

I needed to go to church. It was the last place I wanted to be, but I knew it was the first place I needed to be. I didn't want to go because everyone would ask where Rob was. I couldn't tell them. But still, I knew I needed to go. Satan was doing everything he could to separate me from those things that would help me get through this, and I was determined not to give in.

I went to church, but couldn't focus on the message. I couldn't help but worry over my disintegrating marriage. Rob had called that morning, wanting to talk. Did this mean he wanted to come back? I didn't know. There was too much uncertainty going on. I told Rob that we would talk after church, because I was determined we had to be in church that morning. I needed the spiritual bolstering before having this discussion with my husband.

My father is an amazing man. Where many would get angry and lash out, he saw straight to the hurt of the matter- to the buried pain. I told him what was going on, and he sent Rob a text to say that he loved him like a son. This was out of character for my father, who doesn't normally get involved in our business, but in this, he wanted Rob to know that he was there for him.

I kept turning it over in my head. My emotional withdrawal. Rob's unfailing strength, which failed after all. My need to be in control. His falling apart, finally leaving.

I couldn't sleep the night before. I was not used to sleeping in an empty bed. I couldn't imagine doing it forever. I needed him by my side.

He had been on the phone with *her* all night. What in the world could they be talking about?

I called Bryan at 4:30 that Sunday morning. He prayed with me over the phone, the same prayer I had been repeating all night- that God would make Rob so incredibly miserable that he wouldn't be able to stand it anymore. He'd come home, home to his family.

Sitting in church that morning, my thoughts went in every direction but the message. I don't remember what was said or what the preacher taught. After services, I gathered my kids and went straight to the car. I wasn't in the mood for social niceties this morning.

Rob texted and asked if we were out of church. "Yes," I answered. Everything in me wanted to call him, but it was not a conversation I wanted to have in front of the kids, so I had to settle for texting.

He asked to come home so we could talk, but I'd already made plans for lunch with my parents.

Rob said that he had overheard a TV sermon while at his mom's. Was it a coincidence? There are no such things with God; I know that it's God's provision. The preacher was talking about love, and how marriage isn't just about being happy and in love. It was a commitment. Man was not created to be alone. A woman was created to be his helpmate and companion.

All of this poured conviction into my husband. He texted me, "If I come home, will you help me be the man I need to be? I haven't been the man God created me to be, and I need your help."

This floored me. This whole time I'd been sitting there worrying, trying to see how I could save my marriage, and God was already working on it! I had prayed all night for an answer, but when I didn't see it right away, I continued to worry.

My plans changed in that second. I would drop the kids off with my parents and meet him at the house. I told him to just hurry his butt home.

The conversation that followed was one of the hardest in my life. I arrived at the house- could I even call it my own house? It was the third day since I'd moved out. She had begged me back this whole time, but I didn't know how long that door would stay open. The last time I was this stupid, she said that it wouldn't happen again. She wouldn't take me back.

I just prayed that I wasn't too late.

I hesitated only a moment before getting out of the car. My old life still called to me, but it was only a faint whisper. It had no power over me anymore.

She was waiting inside when I came through the back door, the one that we always used. The moment she saw me, she rushed into my arms. We stood there in each other's arms, and I realized that my cheeks were wet.

"I'm so sorry." I could do nothing else but repeat this phrase. After everything, what else was there to say?

It was only a few moments, but it felt like forever. But I knew we couldn't stay like that. I couldn't avoid the reason I was here. She had to know all what was going on with me. I had to tell her. I had every intention of telling her and then packing all my things. I just knew that she wouldn't accept me back again, not after all I'd done. Little did I know that she had prayed the whole way home for God to give her a spirit of forgiveness.

We finally moved into the living room, where we sat down on the couch, facing each other. We held hands, and it was like a lifeline across a huge canyon between us.

It was the time for truth. I had been so focused on being strong that I hadn't shared how I was falling apart. Like I said before, rocks just don't break- until this one did, and I learned just how much I needed her.

I told her every detail, everything that had been going on in my life. How I was hurt, but tried to stay strong. In doing so, I let the old man back in, and I turned to my old ways.

As I spoke, I could see the hurt grow in her eyes. I wanted to take the words back, stop telling her. I wanted to stop it there, say it would be okay. But I knew it couldn't be okay. I had to tell her everything.

When it was done, I waited. I was prepared to gather my things and leave, if that was what she wanted. But I had to see what she would say first.

She took in a deep breath. Both of us were still crying. Then she looked straight at me, and her next words cut to my heart.

"I forgive you."

Maybe I was a fool for accepting him back. Certainly, some people would think so. The world would look at us and say that he had already hurt me once, so why not again?

I'll tell you why. It's because of God's amazing grace.

Was it fixed? Of course not. We still had problems. I have never been more hurt in my life. Losing a child was hard, but losing my life partner, my best friend, was so much harder. Walking our journey with Faith was made a little easier by holding Rob's hand and having him there to lift me up.

left us, but it was me who walked away. He was there the whole time, waiting for me, but I didn't see it because I was running away too fast.

God has plans for all of us. We screw it up sometimes, but the great thing is that God can use screw-ups, too. He can use someone like David to be a great king, and someone like Moses, who couldn't speak well, to be a great leader. God uses the ones who think they can't be used. That is how God shows His power. It's through the powerless.

We have a new focus now, and that focus is Christ, to let Him run the house we live in, and let Him be the main focus in our hearts and lives.

A few months after this, my wife and I took a cruise, just the two of us. We left the kids with SaraBeth's parents and went to the Bahamas. We never did get a honeymoon, so that's what this trip was for us. We learned how to love each other in a different way, and we were both stronger now. We learned not to be strong in our own way, but to be strong in God and each other.

It was no secret that Rob and I had experienced the hardest year of our lives. It is a well-known fact that an overwhelming number of couples experiencing the loss of a child stand a higher chance of getting divorced. Though we told ourselves we would not allow that to happen, we were almost that statistic. Grief is a hard thing to understand, and men and women, daddies and mommies, experience grief very differently.

We are so grateful to God for intervening on our behalf, and for providing us with Godly friends and counsel, who helped us through our rough patch.

In celebration of overcoming these hurdles, we decided we needed some time together, just the two of us. So, what did the doctor prescribe? It was a Bahamian cruise!

We dropped the kids off at school Thursday morning and headed to Port Canaveral. We were like two kids in a candy store. We boarded our floating hotel, the Carnival Sensation, and set out exploring the ship.

We had the best time checking everything out. We had a great ocean-view room, and soaked up every detail we could. Before we knew it, it was time for dinner. Of course, the food was delicious, and we enjoyed it heartily.

Thursday night, Rob schooled me in some black jack. Can I just say I had so much fun? We stayed up until nearly 2:30 AM and finally decided it was time to go to sleep.

Friday morning, we woke up to a Bahamian sunrise. It was so romantic to stand on the balcony, look over the ocean, and together with the love of my life, watch the sun come up.

We ate an early breakfast, spent some time in the hot tub, then my honey treated me to a spa session. I spent the most heavenly hour and a half getting pampered with a massage and a facial. It was so nice and so overdue!!

We were in port at Nassau, so we decided to finally get off the ship and check it out.

My mom had just been there two months before and told me about this awesome Haviana flip flop store. It was a must-see attraction. Needless to say, I brought home 5 pairs of flip flops for the ones I love.

We only stayed on the island a total of 45 minutes, and then we decided we would go back and spend some quality time soaking up some sun.

It was formal night, so we got gussied up and had some pictures taken. We had tons of people ask us if we were newlyweds. We took that as a compliment, seeing as how we had been married for 9 years!

After dinner, we spent some time playing black jack, and then danced the night away until 3 AM.

Saturday morning proved to be a little rough sailing. The waves were huge, and rocked that ship like a toy boat. People were getting sick everywhere, and they placed barf bags at every elevator. Thankfully, Rob and I were not affected. We were having so much fun, I don't think anyone or anything could have ruined it for us. It was a little rainy, but we spent a long morning in the hot tub overlooking the back of the ship. Then we wanted to watch the Gator game, but they couldn't get it on the TV. That turned out to be a huge blessing, from what I later heard!

We got dressed up for dinner again and had more pictures taken.

We had a rockin' good time that night. The ship was rockin', the band was rockin' and the dance floor was rockin'. We felt like newlyweds so in love for the first time. It was as if we were given a new lease on life.

We were so sad that our trip was over Sunday morning. Though we only got a total of 12 hours of sleep throughout the trip, we reconnected with one another on a totally different level. This was the honeymoon we never got, and it was so worth the wait! Sure we have had our ups and our downs, but at the end of the day, we have each other.

Thank you, Lord Jesus, for the blessing of our marriage, and for putting Rob in my life. I can't imagine going through any of the trials we have faced without him. Thank you for strengthening us in one another, and more importantly in You. May we continue to seek your will for our lives, and may you continue to use our testimony to tell others of the awesomeness of Your love and faithfulness!

Chapter Thirty-four
ONE MORE VALLEY

Just when you think it's all over, there's more to come. I thought I had done enough for God. What could be more than giving up my own child? He *owed* me! Oh, how often I need to be reminded of God's goodness. He doesn't owe me anything, but He gave everything when He gave me salvation. It is so easy to forget!

I became pregnant just a few months after the cruise. We were taking another cruise, this time with the Volpes. Around this same time, yet another test confirmed that I was once again carrying a child.

My pregnancy with Emmy was uneventful, to say the least. With each appointment, hearing every strong heartbeat, my fears withered away. I embraced this opportunity God had given us, a restoration for our family that still wasn't complete.

Emmy was delivered via C-section on Monday, November 19, 2012. It was exactly 18 months after Faith was born, and she looked almost identical to Faith. I was amazed at God's providence in that.

That day meant so much to me, but I had no idea of the trial that awaited. I had C-sections with each of my children, so I knew what to expect. There would be the surgery, the usual recovery, taking it easy for the next week or two. I was determined to participate in our usual Thanksgiving tradition at the hunting cabin, and who could forget about Black Friday?

God had other plans. Almost immediately after the surgery, my stomach started to swell. 11 days after the C-section, I should have been on my feet, still sore, but healing. Instead, I found myself unable to do anything. I lay in my recliner in my bedroom, sobbing because I couldn't do anything for myself or my family. Rob had completely taken over care of Emmy. I hadn't held her since the day she was born.

Finally, Rob had had enough. I was in so much pain, unable to even stand. We were in and out of the hospital, but the only consensus from the doctors was that my bowels had paralyzed from the anesthesia in the surgery. When I passed out in front of my kids after a bath, enough was enough. Rob wanted his wife back. He said that if I wasn't any better the next morning, he would take me in.

At the ER the next morning, it took three different people and nine attempts to get an IV. I was screaming in pain the entire time. Poor Rob was so lost at what to do. He sat in the corner, frustrated. After several rounds of tests, they discovered that at some point during my surgery for the C-section, my bladder had received a small cut and was leaking urine, causing my swollen belly. They drained a full 10 liters of fluid!

The answer was simple enough, relatively. It required another surgery. I wasn't a fan of the idea of more needles, so I asked for a general anesthesia instead. The doctors complied.

I spent a few days in the hospital, but in the end, it was very worth it. It was a trying time, but a worthwhile one. Rob and Emmy developed such a bond in those two weeks while she was completely under his care.

I learned my own valuable lesson in those days, too. It lifted my sense of entitlement. I had given so much to God already, but if He asked for more, who was I to say no?

I find myself taking life slowly these days. This year has passed quickly, but I make sure and snatch the quiet moments. These are the ones that mean the most to me.

Chapter Thirty-five

THE GLUE THAT HOLDS US TOGETHER

Send.

I clicked the small blue rectangle, and the message disappeared into the mysterious realms of cyberspace. I leaned back and sighed. Last one. Had I missed anyone? My brow wrinkled as I considered who that nameless person might be.

Coming up with nothing, I finally decided that everyone had gotten their invite. Clicking the mouse again, I opened the file that I had just sent.

The

Apple

Of Our Eye

Emmy

Is Turning

1

One year old. Our little Emmy was a year old already. Had it been so long? This year had passed with the speed of lightning. I couldn't believe we were just about to celebrate my baby girl's first birthday.

So much had happened since Faith. I discovered that yes, life does move on, but so can we. We grieved, but we didn't have to stay in that grief. We learned so many things, both from Faith and just in the last year. We learned to hold on to life, taking joy in the smallest of things. We learned to let go, trusting God to direct the path in our life.

It was such a fateful moment when we learned of my pregnancy. It was not quite a year after Faith had passed, and I was learning to move on. We all were. I wasn't sure if my family was complete, but I didn't know if I wanted to risk going through it all again.

Mid-March, 2012. We were scheduled to go on another cruise, this time with the Volpes. Bryan and Christina meant so much to us, had been such a part of our lives. We wanted to spend some time with them, just the four of us.

The day before the cruise, I was in my room, packing. Rob was helping me go through the list of what we needed, knowing that I have a hard time staying organized. As we did so, I suddenly realized that it had been some time since I'd had my last cycle. My cycles were always irregular, so I didn't think much of it before. But still, it had been too long.

Deciding that the packing could wait, I went to the bathroom for a test. Immediately, the results showed positive. I found Rob in the garage and showed him the test, hardly daring to breathe. He frowned at the two parallel lines, not sure whether to accept it. These things weren't always accurate, after all.

I wasn't sure whether to believe it myself. So on the way home from church that evening, I stopped and picked up another test. I took it the second I got home. Christina and her husband had pulled into town that same night to meet us for our cruise tomorrow, so she was with me. She saw the test results and we both screamed with excitement.

This news opened a new door in my life. We went on the cruise as planned and came home to a parade of doctor's appointments.

There is nothing like walking into an ultrasound appointment for your baby after you've already lost one child. You can't look at the screen, but you can't look away. You're holding your breath, tears waiting to spill, listening for those fateful words. Your eyes are fixed on the doctor's face, your ears tuned to his voice, listening for any catch, any sign that something might be wrong.

And then he says, "Take a deep breath. This is going to be good. I already see a baby and a heartbeat."

Those words were music to my ears! Never have I been so relieved for good news. I listened in awe as our doctor walked through the ultrasound with us, pointing out what he saw. A straight spine, with all the right measurements. The abdomen and chest cavity, intact. No sign of a birth defect anywhere.

I have never been so happy to hear such news. I cried, right there in that office. I couldn't help but think that this was the same window in the pregnancy where we'd first gotten the news about Faith. How different it was this time! I was so fearful, but it was God who had it all in control. Part of me was scared to death for the Lord to reveal His plans for this child on that day. What if He asked once again for what we could not give?

As it turned out, I was not the only one who had fears. We had another ultrasound, finally determining that the baby would be a girl. Cade struggled horribly with this, and at first we thought it was just his disappointment over not getting a brother. After several days of tears and a bitter attitude, he finally spilled that it went far deeper. He didn't mind having a sister, but he was afraid that she would replace Faith. He didn't want us to forget about his other baby sister! I assured him that we would never forget the family member that waited in heaven for us.

In just a few days, we'll celebrate Emmy's first birthday. We'll get together with family and friends, celebrating the life of my little girl. The theme is "Apple of Our Eye."

It's something of a nostalgic moment for me. I'm so excited to see this day come, but I can't help but think of another day that we could have had, another first birthday party that we never got.

I'm sad, sure. But even so, there's a peace about it. I can think of Faith without feeling like my heart is breaking in two. I don't know if this ache will ever go away, but I don't know that I want it to. Even so, it's not the ache of bitterness, but more the ache of longing, of missing someone close, but knowing you'll see them again. Looking forward to that day gives me great comfort.

Emmy is the glue that has held our family together. She knit together the hole that Faith left behind. There is no way that she will ever replace Faith- they are two separate people. I did not lose a daughter that day. This parting is only temporary.

Even so, my family was not complete. Even before I had Faith, I felt it. We had debated the size of our family and how many kids we wanted, but I knew there was something missing. When Faith went to heaven, that hole remained, that feeling of being incomplete.

Emmy completed the picture. She means so much to all of us. Cade, the protective big brother. SaraGrace, the proud big sister. Rob, the rock that needed a little baby to lean on. And me, the Mama who learned she couldn't be in control.

If there's anything that Emmy has taught me so far, it's that life doesn't go the way you want it to. Just because you've had a trial in the past does not mean that life will be perfect from now on. God is still writing this story of Faith, after all. And He's still writing ours. It's an amazing journey, but one that has yet to be completed. Who knows what's next, where we'll end up? God does, and we have determined to follow Him.

Chapter *Thirty-six*

OUR FAITH RENEWED

It's been nearly three years since we lost Faith. Three years since I fell apart, since I came so close to losing my wife, my family. I can't say that I'm put back together now, but I can say that Christ is holding me up. Without Him, I would fall, as I did so many times before.

We're still moving in the right direction, my family and I. I'm still following God's direction on how to lead my family. See, He's the one that is leading us on. We just follow.

Little Faith will be three years old this coming May. Some may say that it sounds strange for me to say that- "don't you mean would have been?" I know exactly what I mean- and I mean she will.

Faith isn't dead. She's alive- and probably doing better than any of us here on this earth. She's probably running up in heaven right now.

I know that I will see her someday. And when I do, she will know that her Daddy loved her and did everything he could to fight for her life. I can hold my head high on that day, because we did what we could. When the doctors told us to end the pregnancy, we kept going. We kept getting all that bad news, but we knew what we had to do.

This wasn't our story. It was God's, and it was His to write. It wasn't for us to decide the ending. He created that little baby, and it was for Him to decide to take her home. Not us.

I can't say that it doesn't hurt. Oh, it hurts. It hurts bad. There are days when a fist grips my chest and I can't breathe. I still can't speak of her well. I don't want to remember the way she looked.

But up in heaven right now, she looks beautiful. She's the star of the show, I wouldn't doubt. And that's the picture that I want to see when I think of Faith. I know I'll see her- and she'll be whole, like she never was on this earth.

I'll see my little girl again. We'll all be together again, I know it. Christ called her home, but she's there waiting for me and her Mama to join her. Her sisters and brother are looking forward to seeing her, too.

Right now, it hurts. That's a hurt that will never heal. The world moves on, but you never forget your own baby. But I know that when I see her, all that pain will be gone. We'll all be together, and we'll never have to say goodbye again.

'Til then, we're just focusing on God, on doing His will. We work with the youth and study God's Word. We are real people, with real problems, serving a real God.

And always, there's that promise. We will see you again, Faith.

Chapter Thirty-seven

LETTER TO FAITH

Our Dearest Faith,

There are no words to tell you how proud we are of you. You have changed our lives forever. The last nine months have been spent preparing for your arrival, but nothing could have prepared us for the impact you would have on the world.

We will never forget the moment we were told that you were not perfect in the eyes of the world. As your parents, we ached for what you may not experience here on this earth. The next six months brought many emotions, as doctors struggled to tell us what to expect. Every doctor's appointment, ultrasound, even the MRI brought something new for them to help us understand.

But the Great Physician was working in a mighty way to show them that none of us knew what He was up to. Everyone got to witness miracles first hand, as Jesus continued to knit you together, day by day. We were told not to expect to ever carry you full term. But as you grew each day, we were reminded with every kick, punch, and somersault that you were fulfilling God's purpose for your life.

It has been such a blessing to see Cade and SaraGrace pray for you every day. They both hugged and kissed you through your Mommy's tummy all of the time. They love you so much, and you have made them so proud. When they finally got to see your beautiful face, they knew they had seen an angel.

The day you were born, so many people came to pray for you and to see the miracle of life that God had given us. As we waited for you to be born, many emotions overcame us, but the one that we felt the most was love. Love of the Savior, love of our family and friends, and most of all, love of our daughter that fought so hard to share the love of Jesus with so many people.

We were scared of what may come at the end of that day, but we knew the Lord had all of us, even you, in the palm of His hands. As the doctors handed you to your daddy and told us that you would not spend much time here with us, our Heavenly Father covered us with a peace that only He can provide. We knew that you would never know the hurt of the world. You would never have to feel the sadness we would feel when we would have to let you go.

When your Mommy finally got to hold you, we just sat there together and loved, kissed, and hugged you endlessly. You were so beautiful and peaceful. You were so strong. The forty-two minutes you spent in our arms were the most precious forty-two minutes of our lives. We got to see how God's plans would unfold for you, and knew without a shadow of a doubt you would be in a place far better than we could offer you.

Though we are sad, and we feel an emptiness without you here with us, we rejoice to know that God is good all of the time. We prayed that His will would be done. We prayed that if it was His will that you go to heaven, that He would allow you to be peaceful, and that He would give us some time, no matter how short, to spend with you. He answered our prayers. He gave us the greatest gift in knowing that our Faith has been renewed. You are now in heaven, with no pain, no suffering and your body has been renewed.

But our faith in God has also been renewed. Though this journey has not been easy, He has never left us alone. He has held true to His promises, and carried us through the storm. We now stand stronger with Him knowing that He loves us so much, and that He chose us to be your Mommy and Daddy.

We are forever changed by the blessing of knowing you as our daughter. Our time on earth may seem like an eternity, but in reality it's only a snapshot. This life is not our home. We can rest assured that because of the gift that God gave as His Son on the cross, we will see you again, and spend forever holding you in our arms.

But we can promise that this is not the end of your story. God will continue to use us to share how you have changed us all, and we could not be more proud to do so.

With all our love,
Mommy and Daddy

Chapter Thirty-eight

FROM THE KIDS

This story of Faith belongs to more than just Rob and me. It's also our kid's story. Because of that, we wanted to include them, as well. So here is their own version of the story, told in their own words, with only minor revisions to help it make sense. They are children, after all.

"Let me tell you about my baby sister."

"But not Emmy. Emmy is our other baby sister. She is one year old now." SaraGrace bounces in her seat, the not-so-ladylike princess.

Cade frowns at his sister's interruption, but continues. "God gave us another baby sister, and this one was special. Mama told us one time that she was pregnant, and so I was happy. We thought it was a boy at first-"

SaraGrace once again jumps in, unable to contain her excitement. "But it wasn't! It was really a girl. I wanted a sister, so I was happy. But Cade was sad because he wanted a brother."

"I was not!"

"You were so!" SaraGrace sticks her tongue out at her brother, who pouts. Finally, they seem to remember what they are doing, and readjust.

Cade resumes the story. "So then we knew it was a girl, and Daddy said her name would be Faith. But then the doctors said that all her organs were out, from her heart down to her waist."

His sister nods, scrunching up her face in an effort not to cry. Cade takes a shaking breath and continues.

"I cried a lot when I knew what the doctors said. I kissed Mama's belly and talked to Faith, but I don't remember what I said."

"And then she was born!" SaraGrace instantly brightens, forgetting her tears.

"But we had to wait a long time first. I was watching movies on DVD. Gamma, Papa, and I think Grandpa Andy were there. It was a long time that we had to wait."

SaraGrace nods importantly. "But we got to go back and visit. We went into the room two times. Me and Cade went in the first time, and I got to hold her with the pretty dress. But then I had to wait again. I told my Papa that I wanted to go again, but people were still going, so he said that we already went so we had to wait to go last. So then we went, and Cade went, too."

"We didn't get to stay in that room long. I just stayed with Daddy a lot, after Mama had Faith. I took pictures with her and held her."

"Me too! I got pictures, too, because she was my sister!" SaraGrace had to make sure she wasn't forgotten.

Cade shrugs and nods, acknowledging her statement. Yes, she got pictures, too. They all did.

"When I was holding her, I was thinking about why her hands wouldn't move. I wanted to know why her lips were purple. She had black hair. I do not remember seeing her eyes, because they were closed. When I was in there, I didn't really see her a lot. I just saw her twice."

"And she looked like me!" Once again, SaraGrace can't help but add her input.

Her brother shoots her an irritated glance. "No, she didn't."

"Yes, she did!"

"No, she looked-"

SaraGrace cuts him off. "Mommy and Gamma and other people say that she looks like me!"

Having no argument to this fact, her big brother sighs in resignation. "Anyway, so she died. She didn't open her eyes or leave that room or anything."

SaraGrace remembers her tears from earlier, and now her shoulders shudder, lower lip slowly protruding. Forgetting their argument, Cade puts an arm around his younger sister.

"I felt sad when she died. Sad, very. I was angry and sad that she died. I thought that she would be alive for at least a week, and then die."

SaraGrace adds, "I was sad, too. I was feeling like I was dying and then I was sad and I cried and everybody else cried, too. I told God that whenever I come to talk to Him, I would talk to Him and tell him I was sad about Faith. Sometimes I pray about Faith and say, 'God, please let Faith be good in heaven.' I want to go to heaven. Heaven seems so fun, you just get to be an angel, and you get to do- whenever you're an angel you get to tell people what to do, and whenever they do something bad you tell God, and He fixes it. And that's what Faith does."

She jumps up from her seat, carried away with excitement. "She's probably playing with a doggy and playing with some people in heaven. You know, my friend's Chihuahua died. I saw a Chihuahua on the road before. It was so sad. She was sitting down, watching everybody. I was like, 'Awwww...' It was when we were going to the dump. 'Look at the Chihuahua!' I said, 'Daddy, can we have a Chihuahua?' And he said, 'Of course not!' But I want a Chihuahua!"

She's bouncing around now, having completely forgotten the point of her story. Cade looks annoyed, but attempts to continue the story anyway.

"So then we had the funeral. But I'll go back a little bit. When she was at the Milam Funeral Home, Gamma gave me this big bear and I put it in the casket so at the funeral at the church, I think the bear was still in it. But then I also got another bear from the funeral that had a little rattle on it. That was at North Central, and the pastor was speaking about how Faith moved people's lives."

By this point, SaraGrace has remembered the story. She now comes to again take her seat next to her brother, adding her own memories of the funeral.

"Well, we got to have some cake and some real food first, and then we got to have cake. You know I really love cake. And I really love cake and so I had some and we had some children's tables and they had these flowers in them and we got to sit at the table and eat and I got to sit with my friends and that was fun."

Cade shoots her a frown. "But that was after the funeral!"

"But it was still yummy, and I liked it." SaraGrace pouts that her observations on the food had to wait.

With a dutiful roll of his eyes, Cade says, "But first we had the funeral service. But I don't remember a lot; I remember Grandma Sandy."

SaraGrace adds, "It was kinda sad, whenever we got to see her, and I'm kinda sad right now." A sniffle punctuates this sentence to illustrate her point. Bravely, she keeps going. "It was a little bit sad because whenever we got to go see the box, everyone cried a little bit. I remember seeing her in the box, but it was so sad because it looked like she was asleep. I thought she was dead. I was feeling so sad."

"And we did a lot of weeping." Cade nods solemnly.

"What's weeping?" SaraGrace questions the big word.

"It means crying. We were crying a lot."

"Oh. Yes, we were all crying, and I was crying too. And I think I'm crying now. I would tell people that I am really sad and that we will never forget about her."

"Nope, never." Her big brother affirms this.

SaraGrace picks up the story. "Mommy was very sick after she had Faith, and she had to stay at the hospital for a couple of nights and we had to go to Gamma's house and stay with her. She was a lot of sad and we cried and we told her, 'don't feel bad.' But Daddy had a mask on, so I don't know whether he was sad or not."

"When I remember Faith is when I get the bear in my bed and I remember, and I still have her blanket of when she was born. I think about her a lot, when I go to bed I do, about how she talks to God. I think about what she might be doing now."

SaraGrace nods thoughtfully. "I cry at school, too. But whenever I cry, I just tell my teacher why I am crying, and my friends, too. So when I tell them, they say that it's okay if you're crying 'cause she's in a good place now in heaven with God. And she was my baby sister, and I loved her."

Cade jumps in. "But I'm proud to be her brother. Well, half not, and half yes. 'Cause, I'm going to be true to you, when I come to school without her, I have a reason to be upset, and then I'm sad, because I did have a sister."

"But whenever we get to heaven, I'm going to see her. I am sad, but we will never forget about her."

"But I thanked God, 'cause Emmy was born and so I had another sister- but she didn't replace Faith, 'cause Faith is still my sister. But through Faith, God made people believe in Him."

Chapter Thirty-nine

SALVATION

You may wonder how we could go through such a heart-wrenching trial, yet continue to share with everyone how great our God is. It's simple. My relationship with Jesus is everything to me. When I have had nothing else in my life, I have had Jesus. When my friendships have failed, Jesus was still there with me. When my marriage failed, Jesus still loved me. When I had to say goodbye to my daughter, Jesus still carried me. No matter what this life has dealt me, it was never more than He could handle.

If I had to sum it up, I would share with you that Jesus has always been "more than enough" for me.

Does this mean that it's always easy? Absolutely not! Once our lives got busy again after Faith was born, I found myself feeling so distant from the Lord. It wasn't because He had left me, but because I found myself putting Him on the shelf again. In a strange way, I missed the intimacy I had with Him. It was easy to focus on Him when I had nothing else. Now, I felt like such a failure. After all He had done and brought us through, here I was again, reverting back to my old self. At first, I wanted to blame Him and ask why it felt like it was so hard.

But then I remembered a verse that says, "Our God is the same yesterday, today, and forever" (Hebrews 13:8). Nothing on God's end had changed. I was the one who had changed. It can still be a struggle to wade through the daily hustle and bustle and find time for Him. But He always has time for us.

It is my prayer that each of you who read our story would come to know the love of our Heavenly Father. I want to share with you how you can know Jesus Christ. Without my salvation, none of our story matters. If it weren't for Jesus, Faith's life would have been in vain. We would be hopeless, and wandering this earth aimlessly without purpose.

The last few years have contained some of the greatest trials we've ever known. It held a lot of heartache and a lot of sorrow. Yet, through it all there wove a strand of peace and redemption, one of hope in the midst of a trial.

How did we obtain this peace? By the grace of God, as I'm sure it must be clear by now.

This peace isn't exclusive. It's not for special people who have some inner gift. It's freely given to all, no matter who they are. We're all the same inside- sinners before a holy God. That's the first step. We must first admit that we are all sinners. Romans 3:23 says, "For all have sinned and come short of the glory of God." See the word "all?" That means each and every one of us. But God sent His son to redeem and save us from our sin.

He tells us in John 3:16, "For God so loved the world that He gave His only begotten son, that whosoever believeth in Him shall not perish, but have everlasting life." He knew we were sinners. But He loved us so much, He sent His only Son to be born in a manger, to be crucified on a cross, to pay the price for our sins. When He says, "shall not perish," He is referring to an eternity in separation from Him in hell.

But the "everlasting life" He talks about is an eternity in heaven with Him. That was the purpose of Him giving His son. All we have to do is believe that Jesus is God's Son, that He died on the cross for our sins, and to accept His gift of forgiveness.

We must ask Him to be the Lord of our life. Then we must confess our faith in Jesus as our Saviour and Lord. Romans 10:13 says, "That if thou shalt confess with thy mouth the Lord Jesus, and shalt believe in thine heart that God hath raised Him from the dead, thou shalt be saved."

And that's it! There's no works, no "good thing" that you have to do; it's just His gift of salvation. "For whosoever shall call upon the name of the Lord shall be saved."

Once you accept Jesus as your Savior, you will be forever changed. It doesn't mean that your life will be perfect and free from trials, but it does mean that He will never give you more than you can handle with Him. We will all go through ups and downs in this life whether we know Jesus or not. But I can't imagine going through something like we did without the hope of heaven, and the knowledge that this life is only temporary. We have a greater future in God. There will come a day when we leave this earth to spend an eternity with the Father who loves us unconditionally. And because of that, I know that I will see my little girl again.

CPSIA information can be obtained
at www.ICGtesting.com
Printed in the USA
FFOW03n2010090514
5327FF